Randy —
Thank you for your
good advice and for
your extraordinary PRT ♡   **Y0-BRB-503**
Joe
7/20/05

How to Save
for College

The Princeton Review

How to Save for College

by

Joseph A. Russo and James A. Belvin, Jr.

Random House, Inc.

New York

www.PrincetonReview.com

Princeton Review Publishing, L. L. C.
2315 Broadway
New York, NY 10024
E-mail: bookeditor@review.com

ISBN 0-375-76425-9

Editorial Director: Robert Franek
Editor: Spencer Foxworth
Designer: Scott Harris
Production Editor: Vivian Gomez
Production Coordinator: Greta Blau

Manufactured in the United States of America
9 8 7 6 5 4 3 2 1

2004 Edition

Acknowledgments

We wish to acknowledge the inspiration provided by our parents, the love and patience of our wives and children, and the constant support of our respective institutions, Duke and Notre Dame, that provide us with the opportunity to promote access and choice in education.

We also wish to thank Janine Meersman for her fine advice and countless hours of effort in producing this manuscript.

—Joseph A. Russo and James A. Belvin, Jr.

My deep gratitude to Robert Franek, Erica Magrey, and Erik Olson, for their constant reminders of light at the end of the tunnel; Raymond Loewe and KC Dempster, for their vital perspective; Vivian Gomez and Scott Harris, for their indomitable patience and yogi-like flexibility in putting together this book.

—Spencer Foxworth

TABLE OF CONTENTS

CHAPTER ONE: SAVING FOR COLLEGE

Paying for college is difficult for many parents. Next to purchasing a home, it's likely the largest expense you'll ever face. And while there's little that this book—or any book or advisor, for that matter—can do to make paying for college easy, there's plenty you can do to make paying for college a less daunting prospect. We'll guide you through several ways to plan for, save for, and lower your college costs. We'll explain terms and discuss investment and loan programs. We'll cover tax issues and the financial aid process. We'll share our advice, based on our experience as college financial aid officers—and as parents.

We know how challenging it is to send your child (or children) to college because we've been there.

Our Top Ten Messages

As you begin to prepare for the cost of college, keep the following things in mind:

1. After a loving and healthy family upbringing, a college education probably has the most significant impact on your child's future well-being.

2 View a college education as the invest-
    ment it truly can be.

3. The earlier you start saving and planning
    for college costs, the better.

4. Time is your ally; you can make more
    money over time.

5. Be realistic about college costs.

6. Involve your kid as early as possible in the
    college cost planning process.

7. Don't be intimidated by sticker price. Most
    college students receive financial aid.

8. You don't have to save for the entire cost
    of college.

9. Consider paying over time. While this may
    mean you'll need to borrow, it really does
    enhance your buying power.

10. Colleges are also concerned about afford-
    ability; the school your child is admitted to
    will do its best to help out.

APPROACHING COLLEGE EXPENSES AS A FAMILY

As parents of college graduates—and as directors of financial
aid who've helped thousands of parents to make paying for college affordable—trust us when we say that saving for college
before your child enrolls is easier and cheaper than paying for

it during or later. If you can't save for the entire cost of education—and most families can't—work with your financial circumstances to save as much as you can.

And let's be totally honest here. On a spectrum of thrilling activities, most families would position "saving for college" somewhere between "knee surgery" and "IRS audit." Although thinking about saving for college is hardly exciting, few things have such a positive impact on a person's life. For this very reason, discipline, careful planning, and commitment from your *entire* family are critical to making this goal a reality. Remember that this is a team effort; your children are the ones going to school—not you—so get them involved with you, and do it early.

This vested-interest principle makes sense: Students gain more from the college experience if they shoulder some of the costs. Think back on their recent financial experience and ask yourself this question: Do your children value your money more than they value their own money? Hey, does anybody?

Also, your children can use the money they save toward incidental and personal expenses throughout their college years.

Begin the process by having a team meeting. You should agree on a family strategy, with each family member accepting specific responsibilities. Decide on a realistic savings goal that your children can work toward throughout middle school and high school. You might propose that prior to completing high school, they aim to save $1,000 for each year they will be in college; rather than spend their earnings, they can set aside a portion in their college fund.

After high school graduation, they can save their summer employment earnings to cover their book costs and, if possible, their personal expenses for each year in college. Currently, books at most schools cost between $600 and $900 per year. Reasonably budgeted, personal expenses (not including travel) typically range from $1,000 to $2,000 annually. Most students can earn quite a lot in their summer jobs; often, they can save enough to pay for both books *and* personal expenses.

GETTING THE FACTS

A major challenge we've faced as financial aid professionals is confronting the lack of reliable information about college costs and affordability. In October 2003, the *Chronicle of Higher Education* reported that a poll conducted for the U.S. Department of Education found that "about 65 percent of students and 58 percent of parents could not estimate yearly tuition costs or overestimated the costs by more than 25 percent." (For further information on this problem, see *Getting Ready to Pay for College* at www.nces.ed.gov. To obtain current and accurate student aid information, see www.studentaid.ed.gov.)

We aren't here to tell you that college is cheap. It isn't. We *are* here to tell you that few families actually pay the sticker price: It's the net cost of attendance that really matters. You'll read more about reducing the net cost of attendance later; it can be done, and you can make it happen.

A Quick Word About Our Focus

Although a traditional four-year institution isn't right for absolutely everyone, this book focuses on the more traditional four-year programs. Many students approach higher education without a clear sense of how it applies to their future plans. Searching for future career choices requires time. Traditional institutions give students time to experiment, to try new and different things, to figure out who they are now, and, perhaps more important, what (and who) they want to be when they grow up.

The range of opportunities associated with college attendance or post-secondary training are almost limitless. In addition to the more traditional public and private institutions, there are community colleges, for-profit or trade schools, correspondence or distance-learning schools, technical programs, and even employer-sponsored continuing education programs. But whatever higher education paths your children decide to pursue—whether a college degree or a specialized training program—try not to forget that *their* abilities, interests, and goals should drive the choice, not yours.

The Benefits of a College Degree—Money and Beyond

In tomorrow's economy and job market, people who want comfortable, prosperous lives will need some kind of post-secondary training and will therefore need a college degree. The financial benefits are clear: Average college graduates earn significantly more money over the course of their working lives than average people who have only a high school diploma; moreover, advanced degrees further increase lifetime earning power.

This isn't to say that people whose formal educations end with high school diplomas won't succeed—Bill Gates, for example, seems to have done reasonably well without a college degree; however, such examples are by far the exception. The odds of people succeeding in their working lives are greater for those with college degrees and beyond. Here are the numbers.

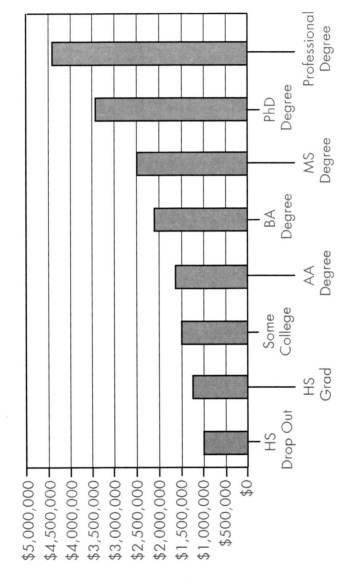

Lifetime Earnings by Educational Achievement

Source: U.S. Census Bureau 2002.

And that's only the *income* benefit of a college degree. Amazing, huh? The average person with a four-year college degree will, over the course of his or her career, earn almost twice as much as a high school graduate with what may well be the same ability. As employment opportunities become more demanding, this earnings gap is likely to increase over time.

There is often a direct correlation between education levels and a number of other positive outcomes besides higher incomes: College graduates are more likely to have access to future personal and social opportunities.

Hey, it's pretty simple: Education creates opportunities. This isn't a chance you want your children to miss.

CHAPTER TWO: RISING COLLEGE COSTS

THE COSTS OF ATTENDANCE

You're probably more concerned with cost at this point—after all, that's why you bought this book. And like we said before, college expenses are daunting at first. Here are some average college costs, as reported by the College Board in 2003.

Average Charges for Undergraduates 2003 to 2004

	Tuition and Fees	Room & Board	Total Cost
Two Year Public	$1,904	—	$1,904
Four Year Public	$4,694	$5,942	$10,636
Four Year Private	$19,710	$7,144	$26,854

Source: *Annual Survey of Colleges,* The College Board, New York, NY, 2003

And while college costs are increasing, the costs of less expensive colleges and universities (usually public institutions) are increasing faster than higher-cost colleges and universities. The 1990s may have been the decade of significant economic expansion, but the cost of college attendance also expanded significantly during this period. Families who are concerned about college affordability became even more worried by reports that focused on the increased cost of the *highest-priced* school(s) in the country (soon approaching $40,000 a year), rather than the *majority* of schools in the country, which charge less than $8,000 per year for tuition. In measuring tuition increases by average costs a more accurate perspective emerges.

About 38 percent of undergraduate students attending four-year colleges and universities full-time are at institutions charging less than $4,000 in tuition and fees, and almost 70 percent face tuition charges of less than $8,000. Only 7 percent are enrolled in institutions charging tuition of $24,000 or more per year. [Because] over half of all students receive some form of student aid, even these numbers significantly overestimate the amount students and their families are actually paying for tuition and fees. (*Trends in College Pricing,* the College Board, 2003, p. 4)

Percentage Distribution of Undergraduates 1999–2000

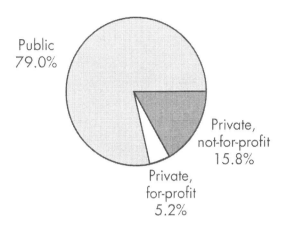

Public
79.0%

Private,
not-for-profit
15.8%

Private,
for-profit
5.2%

Source: U.S. Department of Education, National Center for Education Statistics, *Profile of Undergraduates in U.S. Postsecondary Institutions: 1999–2000.*

Regardless of whether you look at average cost or the cost of the institutions you're considering, it's a virtual guarantee that kids who are born today will face much higher college costs by the time they enroll than current costs. That shouldn't discourage you; we hope your salary will increase as well. But this should encourage you to start saving *now.*

PUBLIC POLICY MAKERS

On another level, paying for college is also on the agenda of U.S. public policymakers, both members of congress and many state legislators. Legislative engagement in helping to pay for college actually has an interesting history that helps to explain today's circumstances. After World War II—as much as for recognizing a national debt of gratitude as for helping to provide millions of veterans with something productive in the face of limited employment opportunities—the U.S. Congress established what became known as the GI Bill, which helped many veterans pay for additional training and education they might otherwise not have been able to pursue. Some twenty years later, in an effort to provide similar opportunities for the next generation of Americans, the Higher Education Act of 1965 authorized federal student aid programs that would indeed open doors to additional educational programs for millions of students who, without such assistance, might not have been able to attend.

As student aid programs expanded at both the federal and state levels and became available from institutions and private organizations, more Americans did indeed move up the socioeconomic scale. Colleges expanded to accommodate the growing demand made possible not only through the many student aid programs but also from the growing number of baby boomers who had been encouraged by their now more-educated parents.

THE BELEAGUERED MIDDLE CLASS

While the median family income may have been growing nationally, many families nonetheless were—by the close of the twentieth century—truly concerned about the possibility that their children's dreams might not be realized because of perceived out-of-reach college costs. Also, many families tended to direct their financial resources to meeting current and growing "needs"—as perceived by today's manner of living. (Whether such spending was from necessity or for other reasons is debatable.)

The bottom line for too many families, however, was that they were saving very little. If unexpected emergencies needed to be addressed, there were always credit cards. (It might be one thing to use cards to pay for orthodontia or leaky roofs, but the cards were too often used for unnecessary purchases.) But not having made plans to pay for the college costs of one or more children added to the growing frustration of many middle-class American families.

Trying to pay for college costs solely with current income, rather than with a combination of savings and current income, would indeed present a serious financial crunch for many families. While expanding student aid programs had grown to tens of billions of dollars annually, by the end of the 1990s, the nature of more than half of these resources had changed from grant and scholarship programs to loan programs. A sense of frustration was exacerbated by the additional incorrect assumption that only the very poor, lowest income-earning, disadvantaged students could receive need-based aid. The frustration increased.

Providing additional student aid through larger programs, albeit often in the form of education loans, did help to offset some of the concern. Nonetheless, pressure from the beleaguered middle class—who were often paying the taxes to support such programs but, ironically, didn't always benefit from them—contributed to moving the political focus away from traditional student aid to tax policy. For these (and surely more political) reasons, federal policy makers authorized the Taxpayer Relief Act of 1997, sometimes referred to as TRA '97. TRA '97 and the favorable tax consequences it created through one of its provisions, Section 529, will be reviewed in chapter six.

Compare the education-driven earnings figures cited in Figure 1 in the previous chapter with the cost of attendance figures detailed in Figure 2, and you'll realize that the additional lifetime income earned by the average worker with a college degree will eventually exceed the costs of college attendance, regardless of where the student enrolls. This very point should encourage you and your children to think of college as an *investment*—one that will help your children to fully realize their potential. And it makes sense economically. Families need to view their total cost-they pay outlay as a lifetime return-on-investment that their children will acquire as a direct result of their college experience.

COLLEGE COSTS

While some of the cost increases affecting colleges and universities also apply to large- and small-business enterprises and state and local governments, many are unique to college campuses. Because you need to meet these costs, it makes sense to examine the costs of attendance as well as the major factors driving cost increases. Call it "truth in advertising" if you will, but you should know exactly what you are paying for when your student chooses a college or university. As consumers, you have every right to know as much as possible about the major decision you are about to make.

Before trying to explain the rising cost of college, it is important to understand the significant differences among *cost, price, net cost,* and *cost of attendance.*

Cost is the amount required by the institution to provide educational and related educational services to students. It is virtually never the published tuition amount. Of course, cost can also refer to "the bill" sent by the institution that lists charges for tuition, fees, and room and board.

Price is the amount published by the institution for the services it provides to the student. This published price is often called the *sticker price.* But this sticker price can be, and often is, revised by various forms of financial assistance provided to the student, effectively reducing the amount to be paid. This can be referred to as *net cost.*

Net cost is the amount that students and families pay after subtracting financial aid. Because financial aid can come in the form of scholarships and grants as well as educational loans, or a combination of these programs (a financial aid package), you can think of net cost as "net cost after scholarship/grant assistance" or "net cost after all forms of financial assistance," including scholarships, grants, and educational loans. The College Board reported in the 2003 *Trends in Student Aid* that a record amount of $105 billion in financial aid was awarded from 2002 to 2003 to assist students and families with post-secondary costs.

Cost of attendance refers to the direct expenses of tuition, fees, and room and board as charged by the school—the cost—and the other indirect expenses related to attending college such as books and supplies, personal expenses, and transportation or travel allowance.

Drilling Down a Little Further

Most institutions charge a comprehensive annual fee for instruction, based on full-time attendance—that's *tuition,* which will obviously be reduced if the student is enrolled part-time (the financial aid package will also be reduced if a student is enrolled part-time).

Fees vary from institution to institution but generally include fees charged to students for various student activities, special technology assessments, and health care or infirmary usage. Major medical insurance can and should be added if your student doesn't have access to such coverage.

It is important that you ask all institutions exactly what they mean by room and board because these charges can also vary considerably from institution to institution. *Room* charges are normally based on a standard double room. Some accommodations may provide air conditioning, private bathroom facilities, or other features, each of which will affect the charge. At some institutions, *board* means plans that include twenty-one meals per week or plans that include fewer than twenty-one meals. Some offer five or six meal plans, and you have to choose the one that best fits.

Book costs are generally based on average charges in the campus bookstore.

Personal expenses can vary and aren't always well-defined. Indeed, part of the difficulty in framing this particular item in the typical cost-of-attendance figure is related to the age-old Latin phrase *de gustibas non dispustandum est*—loosely translated, this means "to each his or her own." We'll cover this particular item in chapters four and eight. Think of this expense as the miscellaneous money that goes toward purchasing toiletries, clothes, laundry, and an occasional night out.

For students whose permanent residency is located outside a reasonable driving distance from campus, institutions almost always use a *travel allowance* based on the price of two round-trip airfares between home and school or the largest city in the area. If you think your child will come home more often, you need to increase your cost expectation accordingly.

WHY ARE COLLEGE COSTS INCREASING SO RAPIDLY?

First, it is important to note the clear distinction between the cost drivers at public institutions and the cost drivers at private institutions. Public institutions where the cost of instruction is heavily subsidized by state-supported taxes have traditionally depended on the state legislative process to support most, if not all, annual cost increases. Huge budget deficits in many states have led to reduced state revenues to support public higher education. Public institutions, therefore, must turn to tuition increases to replace resources traditionally provided by the legislature. As a result of these reduced public subsidies, average tuition increases at public colleges and universities have, in recent years, significantly outpaced tuition increases at private institutions.

Although they are not suffering from a withdrawal of state support, private institutions have long depended on tuition as a major source of revenue and continue to find it necessary to meet increased operating costs with tuition increases. The future health of state budgets will likely play a major role in determining whether public cost increases continue to outstrip cost increases at private institutions.

Public and private institutions are working hard to keep down their costs. That is the good news. The bad news for these institutions and tomorrow's students is that families typically have no accurate sense of what college actually does cost. In fall 2003, the National Center for Education Statistics (NCES) released a study indicating that students and their parents too often overestimate college tuition costs. Other studies have confirmed this tendency—and have additionally noted that parents and students also underestimate the amount of financial aid available nationally.

Remember, if you are interested in any colleges, check out their websites or contact them directly. The cost of attendance and financial aid information you need should be readily available. Always distinguish the *sticker price* published by the institution from the *net cost*, the out-of-pocket cost for the family minus student aid.

WAIT. AREN'T THESE INSTITUTIONS LOADED?

In a word: no. In fact, for most colleges and universities, the tuition charged annually is far less than the actual cost of educating the average student. Remember, the true *cost* of education is never fully reflected in the published *price* of tuition. By almost any market standard, that makes it a bargain.

How can that be possible? First, most institutions cover their annual operating costs in ways that are unique to the marketplace. Colleges and universities devote a great deal of time and energy to finding new revenue streams other than tuition, including fund-raising campaigns designed to raise capital to be invested in endowments. If the gift is sufficiently large, an *endowment,* as designated by the donor, is created. These designations might include supporting financial aid programs for deserving students, creating or supporting faculty chairs, and providing building and maintenance costs. Endowments are designed to be perpetually available. Once an endowment is created, institutions use only the annual income for the endowed fund's designated expenses. Non-endowment support, including annual fund contributions from alumni (most every institution solicits these funds), can be used to support current operating costs. It is endowment income and current revenue or annual fund contributions that support annual operating costs and allow institutions to charge far less in tuition than it actually costs to educate the average student.

Development efforts are so important that any institution finishing a fund-raising campaign is more likely than not already planning the next campaign. Howard Bowen, the former

President of Harvard University, writes in *The Costs of Higher Education*, "Each institution raises all the money it can. Each institution spends all of the money it raises." If that sounds a bit like your family budget, you're not far off the mark.

Although traditional colleges and universities are nonprofit by nature, they seek other opportunities to generate operating revenue. General income is critical to today's colleges and universities. Some institutions receive supplemental revenue streams from privately funded or government-supported research grants. Others may have an income stream from a university-run hospital. Campus activities, including athletic events (if the institution is lucky), concerts, book and apparel sales (it helps to have a national champion), and other sources of campus income also help to support the cost of educating students. Of course, in the public sector, state-run institutions, in addition to these potential resources, annually receive huge tuition subsidies from taxpayer-supported appropriations.

Although the income streams provided by these revenue sources are increasingly critical and serve to help subsidize (that is, reduce) the actual full cost of providing instruction, it's tuition and, for those institutions with endowments, endowment income that are the primary sources of campus financing. That isn't likely to change in the near future.

So Why Is Tuition So High?

A recent phenomenon driving college costs has been referred to (by none other than a congressionally commissioned panel) as *expectations*. This describes what you, the consumers, expect from your colleges.

Competition to get students is as keen as ever, and in this environment, institutions invest in obvious and highly visible academic products for students. It's been said that something akin to an arms race is now taking place on campus. For all but a few highly selective institutions, it's now a buyer's market—and the parents and students are the buyers. Competing schools feel the heat. Institutions that are intent upon remaining competitive offer only the newest facilities and the most up-to-date laboratories, libraries, and teaching resources. After all, students will face stiff competition when they hit the workforce, and they'll need the sharpest skills to be successful in their careers. Institutions also understand that prospective students—as smart consumers—look very carefully at curricula, class sizes, availability of and access to modern technology, professors with whom they will study, dormitories, libraries, extracurricular opportunities, internships, study abroad, and campus connectivity.

Families expect more than tangible services. Consider counseling, for example: If students require academic counseling, such support is, of course, readily available. If students have alcohol or drug problems, counseling is available. If students have personal-adjustment difficulties, sexual-identity issues, problems with a roommate or friend or family, counseling is available. In fact, college students have few problems that institutions aren't prepared to tackle through counseling. While this level of counseling offers a wonderful service, providing it is very expensive.

In addition to costs of competition and student support, the general cost drivers include federal and state government-required (but unfunded) mandates. In higher education, these are referred to as *government regulations*. For example, the campus aid office is now required to confirm each student's Selective Service registration status before disbursing federal student aid funds. Another government regulation stipulates that students can't work on campus without first confirming that they are legally in the country. There are government regulations related to access for the handicapped, reports on campus safety and gender-equity statistics, building codes, the care of animals in labs, waste disposal, visa rules for international students, numerous background checks required prior to employment of personnel, privacy issues, federal accounting reports rules, and audits. You can bet that congress didn't provide the funding necessary to run these federal verification programs.

On yet another level, higher education is a people-heavy industry that must deal with ever increasing *personnel* costs (the competition for top faculty is brutal and expensive) and insurance expenses for health care, liability protection, and campus safety (an increasingly important issue). Colleges have had to face double-digit cost increases for insurance for all of these. Because colleges are often one of the largest employers in their communities, it is important that they contribute to local community activities and needs.

Then there is the ever-increasing cost of *technology*. Students and families understandably come to campus with the reasonable assumption that the institution will provide the most up-to-date hardware, software, and system support services available.

While many of these expenses are issues for corporations large and small, others are unique to colleges and universities. One of our most respected professional colleagues—Gordon Winston, professor and director of the Williams College Project on the Economics of Higher Education—offered the following observation about college costs in a NCES-commissioned paper:

> In sharp contrast to business firms, colleges operate both as commercial firms, selling their product for a price, and as charities, giving it away for social purposes. That a college is simultaneously [like] a church and a car dealer significantly affects the way policies work.

Institutions commit millions to *financial aid programs* designed to ensure that students can enroll, even if their families cannot afford the price of attendance. Considering the various cost drivers detailed above, it's fair to suggest that while costs of attendance may be increasing more rapidly than anyone would like, unavoidable market forces drive the numbers up.

Chapter four focuses on net cost: Few families pay the sticker price of attendance, and almost every family can find a way to lower their out-of-pocket cost of attendance, at least marginally. The final deciding factor should not be what the institution charges but rather what the out-of-pocket expense will be for you. Think "net cost" and only "net cost." Focus then on the enhanced lifelong earnings and the lifestyle benefits that result from a college degree. Yes, attending college is expensive—but remember, it is an investment in future earnings and future opportunities, and it's impossible to put a price tag on that.

ACTUAL COSTS

The United States is blessed with arguably the best educational opportunities available anywhere in the world. Thousands of institutions located across virtually every geographic part of the country offer their own set of programs, facilities, faculties, traditions, and options. Each institution also has its own set of prices and financial aid programs to help students pay for the cost of attendance.

Details on current prices, costs of attendance, financial aid policies, procedures, and program descriptions are plentiful. If you want to read what colleges report about themselves, contact them directly (and after you send in your address, get a larger mailbox). The Princeton Review has a tremendous amount of statistical and qualitative information on colleges across the United States—the *Complete Book of Colleges, The Best 357 Colleges,* and www.PrincetonReview.com are all good places to unearth these details.

WAKE-UP CALL

According to the College Board in its annual *Trends in College Pricing* report, after adjustments for inflation over the ten-year period ending in the 2003 to 2004 term, average tuition and fees at public colleges and universities rose 47 percent, and average tuition and fees at four-year private institutions rose 42 percent. The rate of increase has accelerated significantly at public colleges, where increases grew by 14.1 percent for the 2003 to 2004 school year; private four-year colleges' tuition and fees

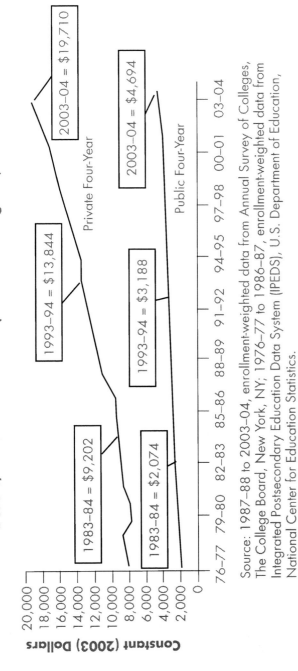

Average Tuition and Fee Charges, in Constant (2003) Dollars, 1976–77 to 2003–04 (Enrollment Weighted)

Constant (2003) Dollars

20,000
18,000
16,000
14,000
12,000
10,000
8,000
6,000
4,000
2,000
0

76–77 79–80 82–83 85–86 88–89 91–92 94–95 97–98 00–01 03–04

Private Four-Year

2003–04 = $19,710

1993–94 = $13,844

1983–84 = $9,202

Public Four-Year

2003–04 = $4,694

1993–94 = $3,188

1983–84 = $2,074

Source: 1987–88 to 2003–04, enrollment-weighted data from Annual Survey of Colleges, The College Board, New York, NY; 1976–77 to 1986–87, enrollment-weighted data from Integrated Postsecondary Education Data System (IPEDS), U.S. Department of Education, National Center for Education Statistics.

increased by 6 percent. The chart below provides a snapshot of the growth in costs from the 1976 to 1977 year to the 2003 to 2004 year.

CHAPTER THREE: DIVIDE AND CONQUER

SEARCHING FOR SCHOLARSHIPS

As you develop your paying-for-college strategy and work on reaching your savings goals, look into other ways of lowering your college costs. Gather your family around the kitchen table and take notes—almost every family can trace connections to possible sources of support and scholarships. Check with your church or synagogue. Investigate any fraternities, sororities, or civic organizations to which you belong. Check with your professional associations or unions. Many businesses provide scholarships for children of employees. Sometimes this support is available only to those who have been continuously employed for a specific number of years, so check with your company's human resources manager.

Have your children research local and national scholarship possibilities. While scholarships do reduce, dollar for dollar, the amount of financial aid your family is eligible for, scholarships don't need to be paid back—and the bulk of financial aid awarded to students comes in the form of loans that *do* need to be paid back. The high school guidance counselor's office is one good place to start; *The Scholarship Advisor* by The Princeton Review details hundreds of thousands of scholarships and provides advice on compiling your applications. Most libraries have extensive sections of financial aid resources—excellent places to find out about both local and national scholarships. You can also check online (try www.PrincetonReview.com, www.collegeboard.com, and www.nasfaa.org). Most of these scholarships require at least an application by your student; others will require an essay or an interview or some other specific requirement.

The goal is to gather as many resources as possible to create a balanced payment plan that works for your family. No scholarship is too small to consider.

THREE WAYS TO PAY FOR COLLEGE

You've got three ways to pay for college: before your child enrolls, during the period of enrollment, or after your child graduates. Most families find it far less daunting and much less expensive if they find a way to combine these three approaches.

PAYING FOR COLLEGE BEFORE ENROLLING

For many families, saving money and/or borrowing are the only real ways that they can afford to pay for their child's dream school. Borrowing is okay, but saving is better for one simple reason: money you borrow is, naturally, more expensive than money you save.

Begin by establishing a savings goal for schools you and your child are considering. Depending on how soon your child is set to enter college, you should consider several colleges, including one or two "reach" schools, three "good match" schools, and two "safety" schools (if that day is still far off, pat yourself on the back for being farsighted—and then conservatively guesstimate your target savings goal). Find each college's cost on its home page, www.PrincetonReview.com, or in the *Complete Book of Colleges*. Now establish a savings goal that correlates to a reasonable portion of the cost of the most expensive institution your student is considering.

The appendix has some simple tools and equally simple calculations. There are also online calculators at www.PrincetonReview.com/college/finance.

Once you have chosen the target school for your savings program, use the *current* cost of attendance to extrapolate future costs of attendance. While there is not a perfectly scientific way of estimating these costs, there are various assumptions you can make. Because educational costs are affected by maintaining state-of-the-art technology and services, providing up-to-date libraries, and keeping competitive faculty salaries, inflation will be slightly higher on campus than elsewhere in the region. You can use an inflation rate between 6 percent and 8 percent to project inflation over time.

Better yet: If you know some of the colleges your child is considering, find out the past three years of rate increases for tuition, fees, and room and board (you can contact the college directly), and average these for your inflation projections.

A similar set of assumptions and calculations can be made to help project a return on your savings plan. Review your savings program annually and adjust your cost-inflation and return-on-investment estimates and, of course, adjust your savings goal based on more current rates and on any changes in your own personal financial circumstances.

Get Started, and Be Disciplined

It's a simple, even trite, statement to make, but it bears repeating because it's absolutely accurate: The sooner you start saving, the more you will accumulate over time.

The best time to start your educational saving plan is as soon as you know that a child is on the way. It's not a bad idea to make your baby's "zero" birthday gift a college savings plan (this works for aunts, uncles, and grandparents as well). Saving early also allows you to develop a more measured approach to your savings program. Because you have time on your side, the value of compounding interest will make a *huge* difference—depending on the interest rate, it's definitely possible that more than one-fourth of this nest egg will be from compound interest alone. Conversely, families who don't start their college savings plan until their student enters high school find that much less of their savings will be from compound interest.

The best kind of savings program is seen and not heard. We're talking about an automatic savings program, whether it involves payroll deductions or some other almost automatic savings program. Stay away from the kind of savings plan that depends on having the money at the end of the month or requires that you remember to take the money to the bank. Something will almost always come up—it almost always does—or some sort of distraction will redirect those savings. Place saving for college at the front end of the payroll process and make sure it is as automatic as possible.

Rather than having your payroll deduction or other savings program deposit funds in your regular savings account, establish a separate paying-for-college fund. Financial crunches occur for every family; if your educational savings are in a special college fund account, you will be much less likely to use that money for other purposes.

By establishing a savings program early, saving for college will quickly become a part of the fabric of your family's financial structure. Ideally, this figure would remain a constant percentage of each month's income, rather than a simple, flat amount, thus creating a structured and disciplined plan—and with enough time, a large college fund. (Later in the book, you'll learn about the favorable government income tax incentives designed to encourage college savings that make this kind of savings even more productive.)

Although there are a hundred good reasons to start saving when your child is still in diapers, many people don't; so the next-best time to start is *right now*. You may not be able to save as much as you would have otherwise, but any amount you save will make a difference.

Saved college education money also takes the heat off of you and your child during the college application and decision process. A secure and robust college fund—while resulting in less cost and reduced financial stress—also helps to reduce the stress associated with the whole "Where will I go to college?" process. Students should choose colleges based on their talents and interests rather than on the cost of attendance.

PAYING WHILE YOUR CHILD IS IN COLLEGE

Just as parents are understandably concerned about paying for their children's costs of attendance, the institutions their children hope to attend are concerned as well. After all, colleges and universities are in the business of enrolling and educating students. These institutions know perfectly well that affordability is an important key to their ability to enroll students. As a result, institutions work hard to develop programs that can help make them affordable. Thus, in addition to tapping into a portion of previously saved resources each year—and for families who are able, a small portion of the current income—there will be a wide range of financial aid programs to help them meet college costs. These opportunities can provide direct and immediate assistance when it's needed, including programs with, as well as without, payback responsibilities during and/or after the college years.

Financial aid programs range from the most highly subsidized grant programs to loan and payment plans with some or no subsidy. Colleges and universities, federal and state governments, community organizations, private companies, employers, and foundations are looking at the issue of equal educational access and working to develop programs that promote opportunity. As noted earlier, more than $105 billion in student aid was made available from 2002 to 2003 from numerous sources to assist with post-secondary costs. Almost every state now has at least one agency dedicated to making college attendance a reality for their residents. Some state agencies offer both grants and loans while others offer only low-cost loan funds (see appendix). Some have even extended their reach beyond state borders. Moreover, literally every state in the country and the District of Columbia now offer a 529 college savings plan, 529 prepaid tuition plan, or both (this is covered in chapter six). More than $35 billion was estimated to have been invested in these 529 programs nationally in 2003, and they are expected to grow significantly in the future.

A variety of paying-while-enrolled options will almost certainly be available when your child enrolls in college. The following programs will help supplement your ability to pay from your savings.

- *Monthly Income:* Once your children begin college, you can redirect the amount you've been saving from your children's fund to the *bursar's bill.* Moreover, you can commit some additional amount from current income, especially by adjusting discretionary expenses during the college years without a dramatic impact on your lifestyle. (Just having your child away at college will free up a great deal of grocery money.) Total these resources and estimate the amount you can pay annually. Once you have determined your annual contribution from income, it's time to consider those resources that can lower the net cost of attendance.

- *Need-Based Aid:* Available on most college campuses, need-based aid is provided to students based on their family's overall financial circumstances.

Colleges use one and sometimes two methodologies to judge the parents' and students' ability to pay, depending upon whose resources (theirs or the government's) they are administering. The Free Application for Federal Student Aid (FAFSA) must be completed each year of enrollment by all students who seek to qualify for federal financial aid, including work-study jobs, loans, and government grants. The College Board's PROFILE is used by many, but not all, institutions as the application for private or institutional funds. (More detail on these forms and the formulas behind them are in chapter four.) Each form has a separate methodology that examines the family's income and assets in the context of family size, number of children enrolled in college, parents' age, and—where appropriate—nondiscretionary, extenuating circumstances. Although both methodologies base their analyses on a snapshot of the circumstances the family presents at the point the application is completed, there are specific differences between the two methodologies. The FAFSA does not consider home equity as an asset and discounts all assets for low-income families; it does not consider medical expenses or elementary or secondary school tuition expenses. The PROFILE examines all assets including home equity, and it also considers unusually high medical expenses as well as certain amounts of private elementary- and secondary-school tuition costs that the family may be incurring. Some institutions require applicants to complete only the FAFSA, sometimes along with an institutional application unique to their school, while others require both the FAFSA and the PROFILE along with their specific application form. Oftentimes, complete and signed copies of tax returns and W-2 forms must be submitted before funds will be disbursed. Prior to applying for financial aid, check each institution's website carefully and early for application requirements, procedures, and deadlines. Note also that because things change (costs, family circumstances, and financial aid programs), you should expect an annual application process with forms and deadlines.

You need to know two things about need-based aid. First, it is generally a good idea to apply for aid at least one time, regardless of your family's circumstance. While some students may not qualify for assistance in their first years, you can learn just how close you may be to aid eligibility. Circumstances change and you may well find out that your children can qualify for need-based aid in their second, third, or even fourth years of enrollment. In addition to the almost inevitable change in the annual cost of attendance, surely a family's financial situation is subject to change based upon employment factors, changes in family size, unusual medical emergencies, number of children enrolled in college, and so on. Moreover, especially in respect to government programs, eligibility criteria and funding levels are also subject to change each year. Institutions are genuinely interested in modifying or individualizing their need-based decisions based on significant and documented, nondiscretionary, or unusual or extenuating circumstances. If there are circumstances that affect your family's ability to support educational expenses, write directly to the aid office(s) with dollar-specific details and appropriate documentation.

- *Merit Aid or Scholarships:* Increasingly popular on some college campuses, merit scholarships are generally used to encourage students to enroll at a particular institution. Although most such awards are based on academic merit, many are offered to students with special talents, including music, dance, art, etc.

With merit scholarships, you need to understand the application procedures and deadlines, and you need to complete the application process on time. Second, keep merit scholarships in perspective. Merit scholarships are generally not a good reason for your children to attend an institution that they might not otherwise have chosen. If, however, your children have already decided that a particular institution or group of institutions provides the opportunities they seek, then a merit scholarship can underline this decision.

Be sure to ask about renewal conditions—such as maintaining a certain grade point average—that might be required to maintain such merit awards after the first year.

- *Athletic Aid:* Historically, athletic scholarships have been awarded to only the most talented and competitive athletes. With the advent of Title IX and the development of a variety of new varsity teams supported by athletic grants-in-aid, such awards are more available, particularly for women. If your children participate in any organized sports other than the more traditional programs, check with the athletic departments of their target institutions to find out what might be available. If your children are all-state, blue-chip football, basketball, or soccer players, you don't need to worry—a coach may move into your family living room during your children's junior year of high school. However, given the exceptional competition and limited nature of such athletic aid, don't forgo planning and saving for college based on the possibility of your child receiving a full athletic grant. Nationally, only a relatively small percentage of college students receive full athletic grants in aid covering tuition, fees, books, and room and board.

- *Other Aid:* A variety of other aid programs can be used to reduce the amount your family has to pay each year, including

    1. *ROTC Programs:* These programs pay some or all tuition, fees, books, and a monthly stipend in exchange for officer commission in the U.S. armed forces. ROTC students are often involved in leadership roles during their college years, as they certainly will during their military careers.

        Although ROTC programs aren't for everyone, they may well be for your student. The substantial benefit of having a good portion of your college costs paid for is huge. While they provide a firm commitment to a job upon successful completion of the program, there is also a multiyear obligation to serve as an officer in one of the branches of the U.S. armed forces. Given their financial value, these programs should be among your options to consider.

2. *Intern and Co-operative Educational Plans:* These programs provide students with a wonderful opportunity to earn while they learn. Although institutions won't generally commit these programs to particular students until after they enroll and have proven themselves, keep them in mind once your children are on campus. In some cases, such programs may involve summers or possibly a semester or more away from the classroom.

3. *Campus Jobs:* If jobs are available on campus, encourage your children to seek them. Students can often find jobs that relate to their academic work or career goals. Most students, including freshmen, have ample time

to work the ten to fifteen hours a week that many campus jobs require and still have ample time for studying and relaxation. It is fair to expect that the average student can make between $1,000 and $2,000 by working during the school year. In some cases, especially for students with exceptional talents or skills, the annual pay could be even greater. While such income won't pay for the entire cost of college by any means, it can provide significant help toward meeting incidental and personal needs. Some studies show that students who work tend to perform better academically than students who don't. While it's unclear precisely why this is the case, having a job requires students to manage their time more judicially and to set priorities, and that can only help. Such experiences also tend to help students learn to work with others, be responsible, and become more involved in the life of their educational community.

4. *Payment Plans:* There are a growing number of educational payment plans that parents can consider. In fact, most institutions now offer long-term payment plans, some of which are interest free. These plans allow parents to manage their contributions by making annual tuition and fee payments on a monthly basis during the academic year. Such plans are specifically designed to allow families to take advantage of their ongoing cash flow. Most plans also provide parents with the opportunity to purchase life insurance to pay off any outstanding balance should either one or both parents die unexpectedly.

5. *State Scholarships:* Not all states offer such support, but if your state does, you need to find out its availability and qualifying factors. Many of these programs require college enrollment within the state. Virtually all the programs require that students be residents of the state granting the award. Check with your state's educa-

tional authority (see the appendix for contact information for your state).

6. *Local and national scholarships:* There are a huge number of these awards available nationally, including scholarships provided by local and national businesses, fraternal organizations, religious groups, unions, parents' employers, and ethnic groups. *The Scholarship Advisor* details hundreds of thousands of dollars worth of scholarships.

Again, such information is available at your high school guidance counselor's office and www.PrincetonReview.com.

A few words about the organizations that will help you search for scholarships: Some are reputable and some aren't. Beware of "ironclad" guarantees of refund should they fail to secure scholarship funds. Some search engines are filled with outdated or nonexistent scholarships. Some of these scholarship search engines lure you in with false promises of thousands of dollars in aid, collect information about you, and then ruthlessly auction this information off to every Tom, Dick, and hard-sell marketing company out there. Don't get sucked in—but don't be paranoid, either. Reputable scholarship search companies are out there, and they can help if you wish to use them.

Paying After Enrollment

Just as you can get a better deal on your car if you finance it over five years, paying for college becomes easier if you can pay for it over time. There is, of course, cost associated with borrowing. This is a cost you want to avoid if possible, especially if you're close to retirement (and if you are, you need to determine how well your retirement plans can handle repayment). But if you do save what you can, take advantage of the payment options available while your children are enrolled; if you find that you need additional assistance, you'll have options to extend the payment periods with educational loans. Some programs are designed for parents and some may be obtained by students; some are government-sponsored and some are provided by private organizations. Exactly what program(s) to consider—as well as what mix, if any, between student and parent borrowing should be employed—will vary from family to family and even from year to year.

Most of these options will become more essential to your plans as you approach your children's first year of college. Although some of the programs may have changed by the time your children are ready for college (especially the government programs), it's encouraging to review the various financing alternatives out there.

Loans Parents Can Consider

The most widely used parent loan program is the low-interest, federally sponsored Parent Loan for Undergraduates Students (PLUS) program. This program allows parents without recent credit problems to borrow up to the full cost of attendance less any available financial aid. Repayment begins sixty days after the funds are disbursed, and the monthly payments can be extended for up to ten years.

A variety of commercial (such as nongovernment) parent loan programs are available as well. While commercial or alternative loan programs are likely to carry higher interest rates than the PLUS program, repayment can often be extended for as long as twenty-five years. Under current PLUS provisions, interest varies annually based upon T-bill rates but will not exceed an interest cap of 9 percent. Private loans typically require more stringent credit requirements and are offered by a growing number of financial institutions. Further direction and information is readily available from college or university financial aid offices as well as directly from participating lenders.

Parents who seek guidance in their financial aid search should begin this investigation with the financial aid office, which typically has done a thorough and regular evaluation of those lenders who provide the best products and services and will often provide you with a list of preferred lenders. To make the preferred list, lenders must meet such factors as quality service from A (application) to Z (final payment long after graduation), long-term commitment to educational loan programs, and general stability in the way they conduct business.

Home equity can often be a family's most valuable asset. If this is true for your family, consider using home equity to support your educational borrowing needs. The rates can often be competitive with or even better than commercial educational loans, and you might be able to lower your costs of borrowing by writing off the interest on your taxes. Others may also want to consider borrowing through other means such as life insurance or retirement programs. Each may have their own particular advantages and disadvantages, and it is usually wise to seek advice from brokers, mortgage officials, tax attorneys, or financial advisors when trying to compare programs. The simple message is that if financing is needed, there are a number of options available, and you can broaden your child's possibilities and relieve some of the immediate, four-year money crunch by exercising your buying power through extended payments over time.

INSTITUTIONAL OPTION TO FREEZE COST

A number of institutions offer families the option of paying for all four years of costs up-front, prior to the start of their children's first year of college enrollment. The family would agree to pay in full the first year's costs at the first year's rates multiplied by four. Because the prospect of doing this could be extremely expensive, the school may also offer a loan to the family, which could require a credit check. The family may want to exercise another possible means of securing the total needed resources by borrowing from another source such as a home equity loan, which might also provide certain tax deductions.

If you're able to freeze cost up-front, great; but be absolutely certain you understand beforehand any financial ramifications resulting from your children's possible transfer to another school partway through their college career.

The advantage of such an approach, especially for those who could afford it and who either might not qualify for or pursue financial assistance, is that the family locks in the first year's costs. Regardless of the institution's annual increases in such costs, the family would have paid annually only the rate charged for the first year. While not every institution offers this option, it might be worth checking into for some families.

Student Loan Alternatives

It may well be appropriate for your student to borrow through the Stafford Student Loan program. Currently, dependent students can borrow $2,625 in the first year, $3,500 in the second year, and $5,500 in the third and fourth years of enrollment. Interest rates vary based on T-bill rates but are generally much lower than the 8.5 percent interest cap applied to all Stafford Loans.

Payment on these loans is deferred until after the student is no longer enrolled on at least a half-time basis, including graduate/professional school. A significant percentage of Stafford borrowers qualify for the in-school federal interest subsidy that allows interest-free borrowing during continued periods of enrollment on at least a half-time basis. Eligibility for the interest subsidy is determined by annually filing the FAFSA and a U.S. Department of Education calculation, which subtracts the expected family contribution (EFC) from the institution's cost of attendance.

Contrary to the too-often assumed theory of eligibility, there are no absolute family income cut-offs for determining the interest subsidy. Students receiving subsidized Stafford loans typically can have up to ten years to pay off their loans with payment and interest beginning six months after they leave school. Students who do not qualify for the interest subsidy may still borrow up to the same annual levels but will be charged the going annual interest rate while enrolled.

Regardless of whether the Stafford Loan is subsidized or unsubsidized, the 8.25 percent cap on interest would apply. Many students who borrow these unsubsidized loans choose the option of deferring these interest payments until they begin repayment, at which time these deferred interest payments are capitalized (and become part of the principle).

Whatever particular kind(s) of borrowing you employ, keep in mind that you're not financing a typical consumer purchase. Most consumer items depreciate in a few years; an educational loan is truly an investment for which there will typically be a significant return over a student's lifetime. Such student loans also differ dramatically from any other kind of loan in that to be eligible for a student loan, students often have no real income history, no measure of income to debt—and there's surely no guarantee that they'll be successful. Nonetheless, literally billions of dollars in these educational loans are borrowed annually, and by far, the vast majority is repaid in full. The low default rate suggests that today's student debt loads are, for the most part, manageable. (See the appendix for an educational debt guide.)

PUTTING IT ALL TOGETHER

The more you have accumulated in your college fund, the less you have to count on current income or long-term loans or payment plans. Again, if you need specific advice on cost and resources scenarios, check with your local college or university financial aid office. While aid officers are not financial advisors, they share your concern about their institutions' affordability, and they are eager to help. In the appendix, the "Paying for College—Identifying the Resources" worksheet is a handy tool for organizing your resources.

CHAPTER FOUR: DETERMINING FINANCIAL NEED

DEFINING FINANCIAL AID

In its most basic form, financial need is a simple concept. Here's how it works: A family's ability to pay—the EFC—in a given year is subtracted from a specific school's Cost of Attendance (COA). The difference between the two is an individual student's financial need, or FN. The graphic below illustrates this (rather basic) formula.

Calculating Financial Need

$$
\begin{array}{r}
COA \\
- EFC \\
\hline
FN
\end{array}
$$

Here's an example.

Calculating Financial Need

$$
\begin{array}{rr}
COA & \$10,000 \\
- EFC & - \$8,000 \\
\hline
FN & \$2,000
\end{array}
$$

This example assumes the COA to be $10,000, the family's (parents and student) ability to pay at $8,000, and the difference or FN at $2,000. Yes, it's second grade arithmetic. But there's more to come—and real life isn't always as simple as this.

COST OF ATTENDANCE

First, let's examine the first item further: the COA, including the direct expenses of tuition, mandatory fees, and room and board if the student is living away from home. Again, some people refer to this as "the bill." But included in the COA are other indirect expenses that must be planned for, including books and supplies, personal and incidental expenses (such as laundry, phone calls home, clothing, and social expenses), and transportation.

Some reasonable and typically modest allowances for such indirect expenses are often determined by the cost of books for a year, projected personal expenses for a moderate lifestyle, and the cost of two round-trip airfares at the lowest rates possible for those who need it. Otherwise, use cost for ground transportation. All of these direct and indirect expenses make up a school's COA.

Please note that this is *not* the bill that the institution's business office will send, which will typically be restricted to the direct expenses of tuition, fees, and room and board. But the COA would be the rough estimate of the cost of sending a student off to a specific college for a given year.

But college costs vary, and they could vary considerably. It's part of the diversity and overall strength of our higher education system. The next example illustrates several hypothetical COA for one year at four different kinds of institutions.

Examples of COA	
Two Year Public	$6,000
Four Year Public	$16,000
Four Year Modest Private	$26,000
Four Year Higher Cost Private	$36,000

RELATIVITY OF FINANCIAL NEED

Now let's assume that one individual from a particular family has applied, been admitted, and filed for financial aid consideration to each of the four schools above. Let's also assume that each of the four schools use the same method of evaluating the family's ability to pay—their EFC. Keep in mind that the measured ability to pay should be calculated in a manner that is blind to the COA: What a family can supposedly pay should be based on the family's resources, not on a college's costs. This illustration demonstrates the relativity of financial aid.

Relativity of Financial Need				
COA – EFC —— FN	Two Year Public	Four Year Public	Four Year Modest Private	Four Year Higher Cost Private
	$6,000 $6,000 —— $0	$16,000 $6,000 —— $10,000	$26,000 $6,000 —— $20,000	$36,000 $6,000 —— $30,000

Because college costs vary, so does FN. At the lowest-cost school, the student doesn't demonstrate FN because the family's EFC equals the COA. In each of the other examples, the COA is greater, so the same student from the same family demonstrates a range of FN—and at the highest-cost school, of course, the student shows considerable eligibility for need-based assistance.

RELATIVITY OF FINANCIAL AID AND FINANCIAL-AID PACKAGES

At the other side of the equation, an institution renders its financial aid decision. Assuming that the financial aid resources to be distributed require a demonstration of need, in each case, the financial aid (FA) equals the FN.

Relativity of Financial Aid				
COA − EFC / FN	Two Year Public	Four Year Public	Four Year Modest Private	Four Year Higher Cost Private
	$6,000 $6,000 ——— $0	$16,000 $6,000 ——— $10,000	$26,000 $6,000 ——— $20,000	$36,000 $6,000 ——— $30,000
FA	$0	$10,000	$20,000	$30,000

At first glance, the most attractive award might seem to be the one providing the most dollars in financial assistance. But look closer. Regardless of the amount offered, the EFC remains the same.

FA can come in many forms. In general, financial assistance must fall into three major buckets: *gift funds* (scholarship or grant), *loans,* or *work programs.* Often, but not always, these types of assistance are put together into a FA package that ideally serves to meet the student's demonstrated FN.

Gifts do not have to be repaid and are typically referred to as scholarships or grants. Sometimes certain conditions are attached to the receipt of these gifts, especially the scholarship programs, possibly including keeping a certain grade point average, living on campus, studying a certain curriculum, playing the oboe in the school band, or other such restrictions. Grants generally would only require annually applying for FA (on a timely basis) and the student's continued good standing.

Loans can come in a variety of forms with varying provisions for amounts, fees, interest rates, deferments, and repayment schedules. These forms of assistance are not gifts and will need to be repaid, usually with interest, after the student is no longer in school.

Finally, another source of financial assistance could be in the form of *work*—an opportunity to earn a salary for a limited number of hours of work during the school year. Please note that when a work opportunity is included in a FA package, it is typically not a resource that can be counted on to reduce the bursar's bill for tuition, fees, and room and board. Obviously, if the student chooses not to work, this resource will not be available. While this source of FA is not typically a significant factor in paying for the direct costs of tuition, fees, and room and board, working part-time can help provide for at least some of the student's indirect costs, especially personal and incidental items.

Sources of Financial Aid and Application Procedures

Once again, a student's FA is ideally met with a combination of one or more of these kinds of aid programs in a combination of resources referred to as a FA package. The sources of these aid programs can also vary and, in the broadest of terms, will come from one or more of three providers: the institution itself, the government (state and/or federal), and private organizations.

Also, remember that the demonstration of FN is an annual process. You must know the deadlines and the procedures required for this annual process. This is especially critical the first time around for a new student, who often is applying to more than one institution. Each school will have its own set of procedures, including its own deadline. Sometimes the deadline for filing for FA is earlier than the point at which the student's admissions decision will be made—note as well that an institution would normally not reserve its limited student aid resources for individuals who might be filing late applications, so it's critical to know each school's procedures and deadlines. It is the family's responsibility to investigate and follow each school's individual application policies. As we mentioned, COA usually increases each year, a family's circumstances can surely change from one year to the next, and finally, on the other side of the equation, FA programs can also be subject to change, especially (would you believe?) if they're government-based: Eligibility criteria, annual limits per student, and funding are occasionally revised. So be prepared, take a deep breath, and re-file annually, on time, and accurately.

Again, institutions typically don't set aside limited resources for late applicants. It's often a first-come, first-serve basis. After that application deadline, while there may be resources, more often than not, they aren't the ideal scholarships and grants but loans.

Keep in mind also that there are a wide range of non-need-based FA programs available that can effectively be used to either replace the EFC or to provide for expenses not included in the school's standard COA. A number of publications outline such alternatives, including The Princeton Review's *Paying for College Without Going Broke*.

METHODOLOGIES

Ideally, determining a family's EFC should be a process that is simple, consistent, fair, and transparent. However, because each provider of resources reserves the right to determine the who-and-how-much for their funds, because each provider administers varying amounts and kinds of funds, and because not all families' circumstances are so simple and transparent, the results of measuring an EFC can and do vary.

There are two major methodologies. The dominant player nationwide is the federal government, which annually awards billions of dollars to millions of students and their families; given the large numbers of applicants involved, the FM does a pretty fair job in distributing (or, more appropriately, rationing) limited federal dollars in an equitable and consistent manner.

Any student who seeks federal FA must complete the FAFSA. Although a paper version is still available, most applicants complete it online (www.fafsa.ed.gov).

Because several hundred schools nationally (mostly private), as well as a number of scholarship organizations, administer their own institutional FA funds (in addition to government programs), many institutions feel the need for a more comprehensive set of data to carefully assess each family's EFC. In some cases, this additional information results in an EFC that is less than that determined by the FM; in other cases, it might be more.

In awarding private funds, especially scholarship and grant assistance, they employ an institutional methodology (IM) to determine EFC. Hundreds of schools and scholarship organizations require aid applicants to complete a form provided by the College Board through its College Scholarship Service (CSS), the CSS Financial Aid/PROFILE (applicants must pay a fee when they submit it). This application process is online at www.collegeboard.com.

UNDERSTANDING THE METHODOLOGIES

Measuring an EFC begins with a number of basic assumptions. This is true for both the FM and IM formulas. First of all, the family is expected to assume the primary role, to the fullest possible extent, in providing for a student's educational costs. Ability to pay, not willingness, is assessed—and the "family" includes the student as well as the parents. After gathering information about income and certain assets, family size, number of dependent children in college, and any unusual circumstances (such as extraordinary medical costs), a formula is employed that attempts to calculate a reasonable family-ability-to-pay figure.

Assuming that a family could use some of its income as well as some of its assets, both of these potential sources of support for the student are reviewed. In determining each family's ability to pay, both income (generally from all sources) and equity assets are examined in light of a number of nondiscretionary family expenses (such as taxes and social security) and family size-related income and asset-protection allowances. These methodologies are applied to both the parents and the student data; the result is the EFC. The EFC, depending on each family's individual data, can range from zero to amounts in excess of the college's cost of attendance. If you really want to get into the nitty-gritty details of both the FM and the IM, everything you need is provided in the appendix.

Many institutions may ask the family for additional clarification on certain items, and most of them expect that the family will provide documentation to support the data on the FA applications, including signed and completed federal tax returns (including all pages and schedules) and W-2 forms from the previous calendar year. For those tax filers with complex returns or separate returns for businesses, corporations, or farms, additional documentation might also be expected. For those parents and/or students not filing income tax returns, appropriate nontax documentation is often required instead. In some cases, this documentation is requested prior to rendering a decision. In other cases, this verification occurs after the decision and includes an understanding that the provider of the award reserves the right to revise the initial decision if the verified data are significantly different than those submitted initially.

(This requirement should not be viewed as a bait-and-switch tactic, since families who are provided FA decisions based upon estimated data are advised that the initial awards are subject to adjustment based on actual verification of documented data. The revised decision thus would be exactly as it would have been initially, if the originally estimated data were accurate.)

UNMET NEED

Simply being able to demonstrate FN, regardless of the methodology used, does not automatically provide all of the financial assistance needed. When adequate student financial aid is not available to meet an individual student's demonstrated need, the result is often referred to as *unmet need*. When the amount of unmet need is significant, the enrollment or continued enrollment of the student may not be reasonably possible.

It's an unfortunate but realistic fact that in the aggregate, FN is greater than the available financial aid resources. Not every institution or organization has all the resources needed. In such circumstances, the provider of the aid may need to use additional factors in deciding who among all of the deserving and needy applicants will receive the funds available for distribution. Such factors could include timeliness of application, desirability of a particular applicant in helping the institution achieve its enrollment goals, the extent of need, in-state versus out-of-state residency, and other factors. Even at the federal and state level, the lack of adequate funding can result in a student's need not being met.

ENTITLEMENT VERSUS ELIGIBILITY

Not all FA, including that from most government programs, is an entitlement: Merely showing up as a needy student doesn't automatically result in adequate assistance. Depending on the providers, none of whom operate from a limitless pool of resources, factors such as academic and personal achievement, state of residency, or intended curriculum could be deciding considerations when rationing limited resources.

Depending on the amount of unmet need, families and students can often be directed to alternatives. At one extreme, students can defer enrollment altogether, attend part-time instead of full-time, or attend a less-expensive, second-choice institution. But more often, students and their families head to educational loan programs. While these are generally available under reasonable provisions, anything that is borrowed must eventually be paid back.

While not all families will be able to save for the full costs of college, the important point—once again—is that *not* saving for college based on the assumption that it will result in full scholarship and/or FA is dangerously incorrect, not to mention completely unrealistic. Virtually unlimited student aid resources would have to be available for this to be true.

The reality is that despite the significant resources currently available, there simply aren't such levels of scholarships and grants. Indeed, much of the aid being made available in recent years, especially at the government level, has drifted from scholarships and grants to loans. Indeed, the College Board reported in *Trends in Student Aid* (College Board, 2003) that two-thirds of direct aid to college students and their parents now comes in the form of loans, and that trend will probably continue to increase.

This is, of course, yet another reason to save and save early.

FINANCING OPTIONS

We don't mean to suggest that incurring educational debt is necessarily bad. Among the investments that people can make in life, few are as important to an individual's overall well-being and success in life as a college education, and plenty of reasonable financing alternatives are available. In addition to the need-based student loans such as subsidized Stafford Loans and Perkins Loans, both federally-sponsored, non-need-based alternatives are available through formal educational loans. Some of these are provided through the government and others through nongovernment sources.

Interest rates and repayment provisions vary, and prospective borrowers need to do their research, ask questions, and seek advice from schools and lenders. Ask about origination fees, interest rates, annual and aggregate loan limits, deferments, repayments, loan servicing, and consolidation options. In some cases, families will need to decide whether parents or students will be incurring the debt. Some families may decide to share it in various proportions.

Other financing alternatives, some with more attractive provisions, are also available to many families who are willing to leverage certain forms of their assets. As outlined in the previous chapter, this may mean receiving home equity lines of credit, borrowing from retirement programs, or receiving loans from insurance programs. Some employers may occasionally offer low-interest loans to help employees with their children's educational costs. For many families, some of the interest for educational loans may be deductible, based on the income of the tax filer as authorized by federal tax legislation. The best advice about what form of private financing is most reasonable for a particular family can be found from mortgage brokers, tax experts, financial planners, or family accountants. Who knows? For your family, it might be cheaper in the long run, after tax considerations, to finance education by using private resources.

Facing the prospect of paying for four years of college over a four-year period, especially for those families who may have more than one student in college at the same time, can seem daunting to say the least. One large advantage of employing reasonable amounts of financing is that the payment can be spread over many more years, including those years of repayment after schooling is over. This is true for any borrower, whether it be the parent or the student. In the case of most formal educational programs, the payment of such loans can be deferred until after college is completed. Opportunities for such programs are often available from many of the lenders involved with such educational loans.

But at the end of the day, families who plan far in advance and save through a regular savings program—essentially making monthly payments into a college fund—would be paying less per month than they would to a lender, however reasonable the financing options.

CHAPTER FIVE: SAVING AND ITS IMPACT ON FINANCIAL AID

ADDRESSING THE MYTH

Of the nasty rumors surrounding college costs, one of the worst suggests that families who save for their children's college education will qualify for less aid than if they had not saved. It's a mistaken impression that only poor people, really smart people, disadvantaged people, or only those whose family incomes are under a certain dollar amount will be able to secure such assistance. These rumors only exacerbate fears that the hard work of saving for college will hinder rather than help families' college plans. And they simply aren't true.

You know what we're going to say next, right? You've got it: *Saving for college and starting early will help your children go to their preferred colleges.*

WHOSE ASSET IS IT, ANYWAY?

So how does the world of financial aid view college savings? Ideally, any policy should be simple and reasonable, be honest and transparent, and provide families with incentives to save. In need analysis, a family's and student's assets are treated differently by the various methodologies, based on the nature of the resource and who actually owns it. Here's how it works.

The Federal Methodology: Assets in the parental name(s) are assessed at a rate of roughly 5 percent to 6 percent. Assets in the student's name are assessed at 35 percent.

The Institutional Methodology: Assets held by parents are assessed at approximately 5 percent to 6 percent. Student assets, however, are assessed at 25 percent rather than the 35 percent used in the FM.

Should college savings be placed in the student's or parents' name? Since it's true that eligibility for aid—federal aid, in particular—can be significantly cut back if you save in your student's name, save college funds in your name.

Again, savings held in the parent's name are assessed at modest rates from 5 percent to 6 percent or less when determining EFC. While this will, of course, increase your parent contribution marginally (and therefore marginally reduce aid eligibility), there is much more good news than bad news. Some years ago, *Money* magazine analyzed this issue. It determined that a family who saved and built assets for college in the parents' name reduced aid eligibility by no more than 5 percent to 6 percent—but importantly, the family retained 95 percent of their savings that could be available to help support their EFC. Take a look at the following hypothetical example.

The Impact of Parental Savings on Aid Eligibility		
	Zero Parent Savings	Parent Savings of $10,000
Cost of Attendance	$30,000	$30,000
– Parent Contribution	$8,000	$8,500
– Student Contribution	$2,000	$2,000
Aid Eligibility	$20,000	$19,500
Savings Available to Pay for College	$0	$9,500

Sure, the family who saved $10,000 qualified for a little less FA than the family who saved nothing—but it's easy to see the family who benefited the most.

Of course, at some far-off point, large enough assets would indeed impact need-based aid eligibility more significantly. But even then, the impact wouldn't entirely wipe out any eligibility—not, at least, until the total asset value is so huge that you shouldn't be applying anyway!

IS THERE GOLD AT THE END OF THE RAINBOW?

Again, don't make the mistake of believing that saving for college expenses is unnecessary because you've heard that FA will be available when the time for college comes. That's not particularly good advice. Sure, FA is available. But because you haven't saved when you could have, you'll either be eligible for less or a different type than you may have expected.

While aid of *some* kind will be available to almost everyone, the issue is the *kind* of aid that will be available. You could find that only loans are available, whether they are parent loans, student loans, or both. While loans can be helpful, they sure are much more expensive over time than money your family might have been able to save. And although more than $100 billion annually in funding is available now, more than two-thirds comes from loans, which doesn't exactly translate into a free ride.

UNMET NEED

By no means do all of today's students qualify for significant amounts of FA, and this isn't likely to change in the near future. Even if your circumstances are such that you will qualify for need-based aid, your student could well choose to attend an institution that offers not enough aid or, worst of all, no FA.

Unfortunately, it happens. Some institutions "admit/deny" students, meaning that colleges may admit students but, for any number of reasons, may also deny the student's request for assistance, regardless of need. Some institutions may meet only part of a student's demonstrated need, leaving unmet need. There are hundreds of millions of dollars in scholarships and grants awarded annually to deserving students who are enrolled in higher education. But again, the majority of the more than $100 billion comes in the form of educational loans.

While this shift from grants/scholarships to loans isn't exactly encouraging, this cloud has a silver lining: The terms of these loan programs are generally fairly reasonable, especially given most students' lack of any credit history, secured employment, or guarantee of future prosperity. Indeed, student loan default rates are currently at their lowest in the country's history, despite loan volumes growing dramatically each year both in dollar amounts and borrowers. These low default rates suggest that the students who complete school these days are able to repay their debts—and further, that the cost of education is well worth the economic and social opportunity it provides.

NEED-BLIND ADMISSIONS

Another less obvious risk could be that your student's demonstrated need may actually be deemed a liability in the admissions process of some institutions. A need-blind admissions policy, while practiced at several institutions, won't be found at every college. This means if a college does not have adequate resources to fully meet all of its applicants' needs, it may decide to admit only a certain percentage of needy students and fill the remainder of its class with only students who demonstrate that they can pay the full COA. Few colleges readily admit to practicing this policy, but if you're good at reading between the lines, find out your prospective schools' policies regarding need-blind admissions—and how they then meet FN.

PLUGGING THE GAP

When the FA available to students is less than their demonstrated need (the difference between COA and EFC), institutions will do what they can to help fill unmet need. Most often, a good portion of what colleges make available will come in the form of loans, including loans designed for parents. But in too many cases, even with maximum student loan(s) and reasonable amounts of parent loans available, a gap of unmet need may still remain—sometimes a large gap—that might make attendance difficult or even impossible. It is, of course, college savings that can help plug that gap.

At most colleges, a significant portion of the paying-for-college burden will fall on the family, regardless of their economic circumstances. Institutions increasingly expect families to have made reasonable effort to prepare for their college years. Indeed, families' proven willingness to sacrifice, as evidenced by their college fund or other resources, is more often viewed as a positive rather than a negative, as institutions attempt to address their many FA requests. These signs of willingness to sacrifice, even in modest amounts, paint a favorable picture.

CHAPTER SIX: SAVING FOR COLLEGE— PROGRAM AVAILABILITY

The Big Picture

In the past, most savings programs were offered by local banks, savings and loan programs, or credit unions. Nowadays, this has changed significantly. Private investment companies offer a wide range of options to meet a family's special circumstances. Federal and state governments offer programs designed to encourage saving for college. Several colleges and universities offer institutionally based savings programs. And in 2003, the U.S. House of Representatives initiated a congressional resolution commending the establishment of the Independent 529 Program (that was organized by more than 225 colleges and universities nationwide).

All of these programs carry with them the prospect of favorable returns on their investments, and many of them have federal and state tax provisions designed to encourage saving. Given all the options available, how do you decide what savings program is best for your family? Start by remembering the basics of saving for college—start early, choose a savings plan that you can sustain over time, consider the level of risk and reward (return on investment) appropriate for your circumstances, be prepared to be disciplined and stick to the plan, and make your program as automatic as possible.

Once you have the basics in place, do some research. If you have a trusted financial advisor, start there. If you don't have a financial advisor, check with your bank or savings and loan to find out what they offer and contact your state education authority or education department (see the appendix). If you have access to a college or university, call the financial aid office and ask for advice. Finally, research college savings plans on the Internet. You'll find a wealth of information on every conceivable savings plan, but do be careful of what you find online.

TEN QUESTIONS TO ASK YOURSELF OF EACH SAVING PROGRAM

Four general groups sponsor college saving plans: the federal government, state governments, the education community, and the private sector. In addition to the above-mentioned savings basics, ask yourself the following questions as you evaluate each program.

1. What exactly are my savings goals?

2. How much time do I have to save for these expenses?

3. Will others (especially relatives) be willing to help?

4. How much risk am I willing to accept in exchange for the possibility of greater returns?

5. What are the up-front and annual management fees associated with the program?

6. What are the tax implications?

7. Do I want to retain ownership of the account, or am I willing to transfer the funds to my beneficiary?

8. What happens if my beneficiary doesn't start or finish college or, for some other reason, does not need the college savings?

9. How do the provisions, savings incentives, and projected outcomes of one particular program compare to those of other programs?

10. What happens to my child's educational dreams if I don't hold up my end of the going-to-college bargain we have struck?

When you have sorted out the answers to these questions, it is time to begin the research; general information on each of the basic providers and their various offerings follows. As always, because these programs, especially those authorized by the government, are subject to change, be sure to check on each program's latest status before making a final decision.

FEDERAL SAVINGS PROGRAMS

The Coverdell Education Savings Account (EDA): Established in 1997 and originally known as *Education IRAs,* this program was named for one of its more passionate advocates, the late Senator Paul Coverdell of Georgia. Coverdell ESAs are essentially custodial accounts specifically designed to help pay for the educational expenses of a designated beneficiary. Coverdell ESAs are owned by the custodian; ownership transfers to the beneficiary when they come of age. Unless you indicate otherwise when you set up the account, as contributor, you won't have control over these funds when your beneficiary comes of age—so be certain that they plan to use these funds wisely when that happens.

Coverdell ESAs are designed to encourage parents and other contributors to help make college affordable for those they care about. Consider the following program attributes, some of which are specifically intended to encourage families to get started early.

- In most situations, contributions may not continue after the beneficiary turns eighteen, and the beneficiary must withdraw funds saved in his or her name by the age of thirty ("special needs" beneficiaries may continue receiving contributions after age eighteen and need not withdraw funds at age thirty). As a way of avoiding penalties if the beneficiary won't use the funds by age thirty, in most states, the ESA can usually be transferred to another family member (prior to the beneficiary reaching age thirty)—and "family member" is liberally applied to include step-siblings, half-siblings, or nieces and nephews, among others. Check the laws in your state.

- Annual contributions are currently limited to $2,000 per beneficiary per year, from all sources. Given that you have about eighteen years to save, it is important to get started as soon as possible.

- Currently, there are income limits on who may contribute. Single tax filers will find their ability to contribute frozen should their modified adjusted gross income (MAGI) exceed roughly $110,000; single filers with a MAGI in excess of $95,000 will have their contributions gradually phased out. For married couples who file jointly, contributions are phased out when their income exceeds $220,000 per year. (Check with your accountant or consult program rules for precise guidelines, your MAGI, and possible updates on provisions.) Individuals other than the parents can contribute if the parents' income is too high.

- The funds accumulated in Coverdell ESAs grow tax free until the time of distribution. They can be withdrawn free of federal income taxes provided the funds are used for a qualified expense (including payments of private elementary- or secondary-school tuition, purchase of computer hardware or educational software, or—in some cases—even Internet access).

U.S. Savings Bonds Education Bond Program: The U.S. Department of Treasury introduced the Education Bond Program in 1990. Series EE savings bonds (issued after 1990) and all Series I bonds can be used for qualified higher education expenses (that covers tuition and fees only) at an eligible institution or invested in a state tuition plan; when redeemed, they can be partially or totally excluded from federal income taxes.

Choose bonds carefully, since not all are eligible for education-related tax exclusions. Series EE bonds issued after January 1990 and all Series I Bonds are eligible for this program. In the 2004 tax year, tax exclusion for single (or head of household) filers begins to be reduced at MAGIs of $59,850 and is eliminated at MAGIs above $74,850. For married couples filing jointly, tax exclusion begins to be reduced at MAGIs of $89,750 and is eliminated at MAGIs above $119,750. For the purposes of this benefit, MAGI includes the interest on redeemed bonds as well as the student loan interest deduction and/or the tuition and fees deduction claimed as adjustments to income.

To qualify for tax exclusion, purchasers must have been at least twenty-four years old on the day they purchased these bonds. If these bonds are used for your child's education, the bonds must be registered in either your name and/or your spouse's name; be sure to list your child as a beneficiary rather than a co-owner of any bonds you expect to use for educational purposes. You must claim the student as a dependent on your tax return the year the bonds are cashed.

Bonds may be used for the owner's qualified educational expenses only if they are registered in the owner's name. To qualify for the tax exclusion, a married bond holder must file a joint return; married tax filers who live away from their spouses could, in some instances, file as head of household to qualify for this tax benefit. To qualify for the interest exclusion, both the principle and the interest earned on the bonds must be used to support eligible expenses.

Additional information is available in IRS Publications 17, 550, and 970 and at www.savingsbonds.gov.

Custodial Accounts: The Uniform Gift to Minors Act (UGMA) or the Uniform Transfers to Minors Act (UTMA) permits you to open a custodial account in a minor's name ("minor" being younger than fourteen years of age) while allowing the investor to retain control of the investments during the fund's growth years. Currently, a single taxpayer may make $11,000 in tax-free contributions annually, while a married couple may contribute $22,000 annually. Assuming the minor has no other income, the first $750 in annual account earnings is tax free for the minor, while the next $750 in earnings is taxed at 5 to 10 percent. Earnings above $1,400 are taxed at the parent's rate until the minor reaches age fourteen, at which time all earnings are taxed at the minor's rate of 5 to 10 percent.

The major advantage of these accounts is that their funds may be used without restriction (although funds cannot be used for parental obligations without running afoul of UGMA or UTMA rules). However, contributors relinquish control of the account to the beneficiary when they reach the age of majority (either eighteen or twenty-one, depending on the type of account and how the beneficiary's state of residency regulates it).

The Roth IRA: Roth IRAs became available in 1998 as an alternative to the traditional IRA. Contributors to a Roth IRA may also participate in a 401(K) or any other employee-sponsored retirement program. Although contributions must be made from after-tax income, the growth of the fund is tax free and distributions, if not more than original contributions, are tax free (if certain holding period rules and other criteria are met). Additionally, with some income restrictions, a traditional IRA can be converted to a Roth at any point in time.

Under current legislation, anyone with adjusted gross income (AGI) below $160,000 per year who is married and filing a joint income tax form may establish a Roth IRA. Single tax payers with an AGI of up to $110,000 are also eligible to establish such a fund. At the high end of these ranges, the tax payer may be eligible only for partial contributions. The Tax Relief Act of 2001 added a new wrinkle, a catch-up contributions plan for savers who are at least fifty years old and who were eligible to open a Roth IRA account earlier but didn't.

Many experts believe that the Roth is the simplest and most sheltered federal savings program now available. Unlike some retirement accounts, contributions to a Roth IRA are made from after-tax earnings. That is the bad news. The rest of the Roth story is good news. Interest on funds is tax free, and because contributions were made from already-taxed dollars, any withdrawals on original contributions are tax free and will not affect your taxable income.

PRIVATE-SECTOR-SPONSORED SAVINGS PROGRAMS

The College Sure CD: The College Savings Bank of Princeton, New Jersey, offers federally insured Certificates of Deposit (CDs) indexed to the growth in college costs over time and guaranteed to meet future tuition and fees and room and board expenses. CollegeSure CDs (both principal and interest) are FDIC-insured by, as they like to say, the full faith and credit of the United States government. These CDs or tuition certificates are priced using cost figures developed by the College Board.

The College Board, an independent educational association made up of more than 2,500 educational institutions nationwide, researches a variety of education-related issues, including the COA. The Board's Independent College 500 Index™, revised annually, measures the undergraduate-enrollment-weighted growth of tuition, fees, and room and board at 500 private four-year colleges and universities. The College Savings Bank guarantees that the interest earned on CollegeSure CDs will equal or exceed the growth of the Independent College 500 Index™, less 1 percent. Even if the College Board's Independent 500 College Index™ grows at a slower rate, the

College Savings Bank guarantees an annual interest rate of at least 3 percent.

CollegeSure CD certificates, valued at $250 or more, are purchased as units based on average private school COA (tuition, fees, and room and board). The price of a particular institution's unit varies based on that school's relative COA. For example, the average cost of attendance at a private institution has been set at 1.00 units. The average cost at an in-state public institution is set at 0.40 units, while the average COA for an Ivy League institution is set at 1.40 units. Prices for specific institutions vary accordingly. If your savings plan targets a particular institution, the College Savings Bank website provides the specific index assigned to each institution.

Bank personnel will work with investors to establish the number of units that will be required to meet their individual savings goal. For example, a certificate for the University of Notre Dame is currently priced at 1.22, while a certificate for Duke University is priced at 1.33. The University of Dallas is indexed at 0.87. At the time this book was published, it's possible to determine each institution's cost by multiplying its assigned index by $28,277. If your savings goal targets a particular type of institution rather than a specific school—the average price of an average public school, for example—the College Savings Bank can help you estimate your unit savings goal.

The College Savings Bank also currently manages several state 529 plans, including those in Arizona and Montana. These plans are open to all United States taxpayers, regardless of residency. For specific information on this plan, contact:

College Savings Bank
5 Vaughn Drive
Princeton, New Jersey 08540
1-800-888-2723

Beyond the CollegeSure CD, a number of college-focused savings programs are provided by private investment companies. Some of these are offered on behalf of the state but have special provisions and various risk tolerances. Still other options exist directly from investment brokers. Fidelity Investments, for example, is currently involved with a number of state programs but would also offer its own private plans. Websites for these options as well as for other sources of information on saving for college appear in the appendix.

INSTITUTIONAL SAVINGS PROGRAMS

Increasingly concerned about the affordability issue, many educational institutions have developed savings or savings-like programs. These include prepaid tuition-certificate plans similar to those sponsored by state education authorities (discussed in the next chapter) and plans that allow a family to pay for four years of tuition up-front at either a discounted rate or one that locks in tuition rates at the current freshmen rate. Contact individual institutions for specific details regarding any such plans that they might offer.

CHAPTER SEVEN: 529 PROGRAMS

STATE-SPONSORED SAVINGS PROGRAMS

The Taxpayer Relief Act of 1997 (TRA '97) contained a provision, Section 529, providing a tax-advantaged savings program specifically for higher education expenses: A Qualified Tuition Program could be established by a state, an agency, or organization contracted by a state under which a person could invest in a program intended for saving for college for an individual beneficiary.

Such a program could be in the form of a prepaid plan *or* a savings plan. Although these 529 programs would be established and administered at the state level, there would be favorable federal income tax provisions made available. Nothing legislated in the federal code precluded the state from also offering certain state and local income tax relief, and several states have since indeed provided at least limited state and local tax relief based upon the amounts invested in these programs each year by state resident taxpayers. Virtually every state in the country, including the District of Columbia now offers either a prepaid tuition program or a savings plan. Some offer both.

$400 BILLION COULDN'T BE WRONG

The establishment of 529 programs across the country provides many families a great opportunity to help make college more affordable. It's a relatively simple solution—and a far less burdensome one than waiting until the day when the first college bill arrives. Parents, grandparents, godparents, relatives, or friends can open such accounts for future college students, and funds are controlled by the account owner. Some state 529 programs provide additional incentives beyond the federal tax provisions (at least one state offers a lottery among new 529 contributors from which the agency awards college scholarships to beneficiaries of its program). For contributors meeting certain conditions in some state programs, such as family income or the age of the beneficiary (among other requirements), matching contributions are made by the state agency to the beneficiary's fund. Generally, some programs allow contributors to start with payments as small as $25. Indeed, a growing number of employers provide an option for an automated payroll deduction for college savings programs.

When education is viewed as the investment it should be, engaging in a 529 program is a great savings tool, although it may affect financial aid later on. Again, with more than two-thirds of direct aid coming in the form of loans, it bears repeating: the best and most often least-expensive way to pay is to start saving at the earliest possible date, ideally at the birth of the future student, rather than borrowing later. And 529 programs are popular; estimates of up to $400 billion invested in them are projected by 2010.

So what's the difference between a 529 Prepaid Tuition Plan and a 529 College Savings Plan?

529 Prepaid Tuition Plan

Under a 529 Prepaid Tuition Plan (versus a 529 College Savings Plan), a person may purchase tuition credits or certificates on behalf of a designated beneficiary. These certificates or tuitions credits entitle the beneficiary to waive payment of tuition expenses—*not* room and board and, in some states, not books—at eligible institutions (this prepaid program does not guarantee admission to college). The purchaser buys a portion of tuition at today's price and is guaranteed an equivalent amount of the beneficiary's future tuition costs, thus offering the buyer a solid peace of mind. So if one purchases a certificate for one year of full tuition today—at today's price—for a given institution, that certificate, presented eighteen years later at that institution, would be worth the *full price of tuition* at the time of enrollment. A certificate, purchased today, whose value was 15 percent of today's tuition at a particular institution would likewise be worth 15 percent of tuition eighteen years later upon enrollment.

Because tuition costs vary from school to school, so would the proportion covered by a given certificate. For example, a $2,000 certificate might cover 25 percent of one year's cost for one institution, but the same $2,000 certificate might be 33 percent of another school's tuition. A prepaid tuition program generally applies to tuition at an in-state public institution and may cover some other expenses as well. More states now also allow the beneficiary to take the value of the prepaid tuition benefit to private institutions and out-of-state colleges, but not always at full value. A major difference between a 529 Prepaid Tuition Plan and a 529 College Savings Plan is that the prepaid program most often provides a guarantee and allows the purchaser to lock in future tuition at current prices. Prepaid tuition programs are generally easy to understand and involve little risk, as they are backed by the full faith and credit of the state.

An attractive feature of a 529 Prepaid Tuition Plan is its ability to provide a hedge against bad economic times. Recent state budgetary problems, for example, have reduced state subsidies to higher education institutions and forced rather steep tuition increases in many states. This scenario isn't unusual when the economy is on a downturn. So when other forms of savings and investments are declining and not able to keep up with tuition increases, the value of prepaid tuition plans remain guaranteed. And actually, in a couple of states, this guarantee has forced the state's 529 Prepaid Tuition Plan to suspend (temporarily, in most cases) new contributions. While the return of such an investment may not always be able to produce the highest return, it is often a safe, affordable, easy, and tax-exempted way of doing so, especially for those of us who do not have the expertise, time, or money to invest on our own.

As always, the chance for greater returns most often comes with an equal proportion of risk. Although 529 College Savings Plans, as compared to 529 Prepaid Tuition Plans, may be more flexible and provide greater returns, they don't offer any guarantees.

529 COLLEGE SAVINGS PLAN

In a 529 College Savings Plan, a person may make contributions to an account that is established to meet the qualified higher education expenses (the "qualified" expenses vary from state to state) of the designated beneficiary. The simple intent of the program is that the return on the investment made will equal or exceed the rate of increase in college costs over the years between the time the account is established and the time for paying college bills arrives. However, although some states may provide for a minimal return on the investment you may make in their 529 College Savings Plan, most will neither ensure nor guarantee a positive return. Amounts invested and returns are thus subject to fluctuation, including general market conditions.

Some of the college savings programs offered by states do provide a limited array of options or investment choices ranging from conservative to aggressive. Some also allow the investor's decisions to be revised annually. Under federal law, however, account owners of state-sponsored tuition savings programs may not exercise any specific investment direction. Other investment provisions outlined in the federal law do allow the state to offer broad but limited investment options. Most 529 College Savings Plans provide some range of asset allocation options that purchasers may want to consider, based upon the age of the beneficiary or the number of years until college enrollment. A savings plan for a younger child might, for example, begin with a more aggressive strategy that gradually becomes more conservative as the college years approach. Again, however, no account owner, contributor, or designated beneficiary may directly or indirectly control the daily investment decisions of any amounts attributable to contributions. Most 529 College Savings Plans permit the beneficiary to take the full value of the investment to any college in the United

States, including to some affiliated study abroad programs. But again, as with any such investment program, a 529 College Savings Plan does involve market risk.

THE FAVORABLE TAX CONCEPT

Both state 529 plans—prepaid tuition and college savings—have favorable federal income tax provisions that enhance the prospects of achieving greater returns than would otherwise result were federal taxes incurred. In addition to the requirement that the program be established and maintained by a state, it also must be targeted for higher education expenses—tuition (sans room and board), in the case of a 529 Prepaid Tuition Plan, and whichever expenses are considered qualified by the state, in the case of a 529 College Savings Plan. Payments to these 529 programs must be in the form of cash contributions (direct transfers of stock would not be permitted). If the purchaser requested a refund from a 529 plan for a use other than what had initially been planned—that is, qualified higher education expenses—he or she would incur a tax penalty. The state is also required to follow certain standards in keeping separate accounting and is limited in a number of other ways by the federal law. Typically there are no application, maintenance, or transaction fees other than a modest management fee that would cover all of the program's costs.

SOME BROAD OBSERVATIONS

When compared to many other alternatives, such as the Uniform Gift to Minors Accounts (UGMAs) and Coverdell Education Savings Accounts (ESAs), 529 programs do offer considerable advantages—including a provision for rolling over the proceeds of one 529 program to another 529 program without penalty.

These observations are to be viewed only in the broadest of terms; because the authors aren't tax experts, more specific details about 529 programs are left unsaid. Also, the issues and provisions involved in many of these state programs do vary by state and are subject to periodic change. Indeed, many of these programs are evolving even at the time of writing. Although 529 programs will likely be around for many years to come, it is important to note that the recession from 2001 to 2003 has caused a small number of states to review and in some cases, recast, or even suspend some aspects of their programs. It's best to suggest going directly to each state's website for the most up-to-date information; the appendix provides information on finding these sites. Of course, you should also seek the advice of a tax advisor or certified financial planner. Likewise, whether a 529 Prepaid Tuition Plan or College Savings Plan is a better route than to some other paying-for-college plans, is ultimately a decision that depends on the person's total financial circumstances, net worth, age, unusual family obligations, number and age of children, health considerations, tax bracket, retirement and estate issues, and other such factors.

COORDINATION WITH CERTAIN OTHER FEDERAL TAX BENEFITS

The TRA '97 also created tax credits and tax deductions for the payment of tuition and fees (not room and board) under certain conditions and within a number of limitations, including income caps on eligibility. The student whose tuition and fees are being used to request the tax credit must be claimed as a dependent on the tax filer's federal tax return. These programs are known as the federal Hope Scholarship Tax Credit and the Lifetime Learning Tax Credit.

Here's how each works. Individuals who pay tuition and fees may claim a Hope Scholarship Tax Credit of up to $1,500 per year for the first two years that a student is enrolled in college. Likewise, individuals paying tuition and fees during the third and fourth years of enrollment may claim a tax credit of $1,000 per year. Taxpayers who meet certain income limitations may claim the Hope Scholarship Tax Credit and the Lifetime Learning Tax Credit. These particular tax benefits have nothing directly to do with saving for college because federal policy-makers authorized these two tax credits as an indirect means of helping qualified families with college costs, but they can be an important aspect of your overall paying-for-college strategy.

For families who save by using 529 plans, some financial planning will be necessary. The Hope Scholarship and Lifetime Learning Tax Credits of TRA '97 can be claimed in the same tax year that a tax exempt 529 distribution is taken, but the distribution may not be used for the same qualified higher education expenses. In other words, a taxpayer cannot gain more than one tax benefit for the exact same educational expenses on a tax return. Thus, if a tax-favored 529 disbursement covered full tuition and fees in a given tax year, then that tuition payment could not also be considered for a Hope tax credit for the same year. However, if a 529 disbursement covered only part of the tuition and fees, then at least part of the remaining balance of those costs could be considered for a federal tuition and fees tax credit through the federal Hope Scholarship or Lifetime Learning provisions.

The Hope Scholarship and Lifetime Learning Tax Credits were first made available in 1998. Because the timing of these benefits involves reimbursements after tuition and fees have been paid, some observers might argue that they are not available when funds are needed to meet the actual obligations for the payment of college costs. Nonetheless, these education tax credits exceeded $5 billion in 2002 and do provide helpful assistance to families in the long term. They have grown to now represent more than 5 percent of the student aid resources estimated as available to help meet college costs.

THE TUITION AND FEES TAX DEDUCTION

Another tax provision allows for a tax deduction for tuition and fees if certain conditions are met. These conditions include having paid qualified tuition and fees at an eligible institution. This deduction may currently be up to $3,000 per year and can reduce the amount of your taxable income (this has a phase-out based on adjusted gross income; and if the parents are married and filing jointly, they can't take the deduction if their joint adjusted gross income is over $130,000). This deduction is available even for tax filers who do not itemize deductions on Schedule A, and the understandings for these terms are similar to those defining eligibility for other education tax benefits. Once again, there is the provision that restricts the taxpayer from claiming any form of favorable tax benefit for the same payment more than once in a given calendar year.

529 Benefits

In an effort to encourage families to save for their children's college expenses, congress developed the Section 529 Plan. 529 plans provide some rather attractive benefits. A major advantage is the opportunity to save and pay for qualified higher education expenses free from federal (and in at least some cases, state) taxes. 529 assets grow free of these taxes and can also be distributed without such tax liability.

For those individuals with larger estates (grandparents), there could be significant reductions in the taxation of these assets if they had been used to purchase 529 plans—and what greater support can a grandparent provide than the gift of education? Indeed, many also find the favorable tax treatment of 529 plans a good estate planning device for the following reasons:

- They offer favorable federal estate and gift tax provisions.

- They allow you to average gifts of more than $11,000 per beneficiary ($22,000 for married couples) over a five-year period.

- They provide up to $55,000 ($110,000 per couple) contribution in one year with the condition that no additional gifts can be made during a five-year period (beyond that, contributions are taxable).

- They immediately remove such contributions below annual estate-reduction limits from donor's gross taxable estate.

Another major benefit of 529 programs, especially in comparison with other accounts such as UGMAs and Coverdell ESAs, is that the purchaser has control with respect to how the asset will be used, even after it has been given away. These 529 plans offer what many believe is the most advantageous program for planning for college costs available today. These plans feature favorable tax treatment, owner control, owner withdrawals (with penalties, of course), realistic savings limits, some investment flexibility, and the opportunity for multiple investors, that is, virtually anyone can invest on the beneficiary's behalf. Here are the important points.

Favorable Tax Treatment: Investments in 529 plans are free from additional federal income taxation. Account earnings are tax-deferred and exempt from annual capital gains taxes and ordinary income taxes. Funds used to pay qualified costs of education (tuition, fees, room, board, books, and supplies) are exempt from federal taxes and often free from state taxes as well. State tax treatments vary from state to state, so check each plan carefully.

Owner Control: Unlike the UGMAs discussed earlier, the 529 account does not become the property of the beneficiary. Owners never lose control and may withdraw the funds at any point, although they will be charged interest and a penalty—generally 10 percent—for early withdrawal. Moreover, at any point, account owners may change the name of the beneficiary. There is no limit on how long 529 investments may remain in place. This is particularly important if the beneficiary might go to school later.

More important, 529 funds may be used for undergraduate, graduate, or professional studies at any accredited degree-granting institution, public or private (if you're saving for graduate studies, keep in mind there's frequently less financial aid available at the grad level than at the undergrad level). This may be one the 529 plans' most important benefits—although families should focus their savings efforts on supporting undergraduate expenses, since in graduate school, students are viewed as independent and can therefore qualify for assistance without respect to their family's circumstance.

Realistic Savings Limits: Unlike Coverdell and some other college savings accounts, 529 programs place no annual limit on contributions; rather, they limit only the total amount that may be invested in each fund. Investment limits vary from state to state, with most states setting these limits at the total cost of attending undergraduate and graduate school at the most expensive institution in the state. If there is a medical school in your state, the total cost of obtaining both a baccalaureate and a medical degree are likely to be the state's 529 target savings figure.

Investment Flexibility: Some state 529 plans offer a variety of investment options from which to choose. North Carolina, for example, offers three investment options—one with low-risk investments, one with moderate risks, and one with high risk. Potential returns and, of course, losses vary accordingly.

Some states offer age-based investment programs structured so that each certificate's value changes as the beneficiary ages.

Investors may contribute to both a 529 plan and a Coverdell ESA each year for the same beneficiary.

Multiple Investors: There are no restrictions on who can invest in a beneficiary's 529 account. This, of course, means that parents and grandparents, aunts, uncles, cousins, and even your good neighbor, Bob, can invest. Because anyone may invest, Section 529 accounts, more than any other college savings plan, encourage the entire family to participate in making a difference for their beneficiary.

Comparison Between 529 and Coverdell Savings Plans

	529	Coverdell
Who can contribute?	Anyone	Anyone
Annual Contribution Limit	Generous limits *	$2,000 per child
Account Owner	Purchaser	At age eighteen, becomes beneficiary's
Age of Beneficiary	Any age	Birth to age eighteen
Taxes on Qualified Withdrawals	No federal	No federal
Timing of Withdrawals	Whenever beneficiary goes to college	Beneficiary between ages eighteen to thirty
Income Restrictions	None	Couples' income must be less than $220,000

*See Appendix A

Generally, Coverdell ESAs are more restrictive in several ways including amounts, the timeframe within which they must be used, and family income criteria; moreover, they provide less control and contain many conditions not found in 529 programs. Also, some of the Coverdell rules can be confusing and may become even more so with future revisions to the tax code.

A major feature of 529 programs is the tax advantage provided through the power of federal tax-free interest compounding, resulting in dramatic differences, especially over longer periods of time. Rather than paying taxes on these funds, these dollars remain as part of the fund and are reinvested. Assuming a $5,000 annual investment with an average annual return of 8 percent and a federal income tax rate of 28 percent, investments made in a federal tax-free 529 plan will yield, in eighteen years, $202,231. The same investment placed in a taxable fund will, in the same eighteen years, yield only $159,762. The difference is huge.

When compared to other forms of savings instruments, 529 plans also offer additional opportunities. These include much greater flexibility, depending on the state program, on the amount that can be contributed annually. The beneficiary could be of any age and the benefit is available whenever the beneficiary goes to college. Finally, there is no income restriction on individuals who seek to participate in a 529 program, and other individuals (aunts, uncles, or grandparents) can also contribute to the 529 account you establish. Moreover, individuals can open as many accounts as they wish (but each account can have only one beneficiary).

The beneficiary must be at least one day old and have a social security number within 180 days of having been enrolled in a 529 account. While an account can only have one designated beneficiary, a parent, for example, could open an account for one child and later change the beneficiary to another member of the child's family. With most programs, a minimum period is required (for example, thirty-six months) before funds can be withdrawn for qualified expenses without a penalty. The earlier the account is established, the more time there will be to save, take advantage of the tax exemption, and to be prepared to support college expenses. A 529 contribution could serve as an ideal birthday or holiday gift, since there are typically no requirements that the beneficiary be a tax dependent of the purchaser. Although there is some variance in the rules from state to state, generally the proceeds of a 529 account can be used at all accredited institutions of higher education in the United States, including undergraduate, graduate, post-graduate, vocational, and eligible study-abroad programs. Depending on the type of 529 program (prepaid or college savings), qualified higher education expenses currently could include tuition, fees, room, board, books, and supplies (personal and transportation costs are not included). Students attending on a less than full-time basis may have tuition included, but if they are part-time, not their room and board. Finally, it is also important to note that even though the federal tax code authorizes using 529 College Savings Plans for expenses other than tuition and fees, 529 Prepaid Tuition Plans may restrict their programs to only tuition and fees. Some might also limit the amount of the tuition and fees that can be considered.

Some of the qualifying higher education expenses for 529 College Savings Plan benefits include

- tuition, fees, supplies, books, and equipment required for enrollment

- most room and board expenses, assuming full-time student status

- eligible undergraduate, graduate or professional institutions

- traditional institutions of higher education or approved business, trade, technical or other occupational schools

Again, each state may decide on certain additional restrictions—that is, calculating limitations on amounts based upon actual costs at actual state schools. Or such limits may be triggered when the total value of an account reaches the maximum set by the state. But such maximums are typically quite generous and again pertain to each beneficiary, thus allowing a purchaser to establish accounts for multiple individuals. Also important to note is that many states will not consider these 529 accounts in determining the student's eligibility for their state-administered financial aid programs. However, federal and institutional programs might consider these in some manner when determining eligibility (see chapter five).

WITHDRAWALS

Funds may be withdrawn tax-free and used to pay qualified education costs. If for some reason they are withdrawn and are used in some other, nonqualified way, there is a tax consequence plus a 10 percent penalty on the earnings that have accrued. However, exceptions are made in the case of death, disability, or the beneficiary's receipt of scholarship assistance in an amount that offsets all qualified education costs (for example, an appointment to the U.S. Naval Academy or a full athletic grant to Duke University or Notre Dame College). In such circumstances, while earnings are taxed, there is no penalty. The other way funds may be withdrawn is through a rollover to another 529 account.

Here are four ways to get your money out of a 529 plan. (Remember, too, that the flexibility of a 529 can help mitigate future uncertainty.)

- qualified: free from federal and (most) state taxes

- nonqualified: tax plus 10 percent penalty on earnings

- nonqualified with exception: tax on earnings, no penalty (in cases of death, disability, or scholarship)

- rollover

While many of these flexible provisions for use did not exist in the earlier versions of 529 programs, their growing popularity and expansion nationwide have combined to produce some rather keen competition among programs. As is often the case when the market reacts to such competition, consumers benefit and more generous provisions result. In the case of 529 accounts, this competition has led to higher savings limits, improved tax benefits, broadened use of the proceeds, out-of-state portability, opportunities in some states for purchase by out-of-state residents, and the ability to change beneficiaries. At least one state allows investors to keep the program even if they move to another state. However, some states require that either the account owner or the beneficiary be a state resident when the account is opened. Indeed, if a particular state program does not offer the level of flexibility you believe appropriate, then you or the investor might want to look into other programs that do.

The information found in the appendix of this book will allow you to make some of these broad comparisons. However, because things can and do change, and because it's usually wise to drill down further into the details, you should investigate individual programs thoroughly. The appendix also provides website addresses for such further review. The most current provisions will be found on each program's actual website; also check www.savingforcollege.com or www.collegesavings.org for specific state programs.

CHANGE OF BENEFICIARY

Beneficiaries can be changed without income tax consequences within certain constraints (transfers may be subject to gift taxes): the new beneficiary must be a member of the family, as defined in the law, of the current beneficiary. A member of the family of the beneficiary—not of the purchaser—includes the following:

- a son or daughter (natural or legally adopted), or a descendent of either

- a stepson or stepdaughter

- a brother or sister (by whole or half-blood), or a stepbrother or stepsister

- the father or mother, or an ancestor of either

- a stepfather or stepmother

- a niece or nephew

- an aunt or uncle

- a son-in-law, daughter-in-law, father-in-law, mother-in-law, brother-in-law, or sister-in-law

- the spouse of the designated beneficiary or the spouse of any of the relatives listed above

- first cousins (although a spouse of a first cousin would not qualify)

While some states may further restrict such transfers, they cannot expand this list of beneficiaries. Indeed, 529 programs provide considerable flexibility in addition to considerable tax benefits.

Again, Section 529 Plans are now offered by every state in the union including the District of Columbia and by any number of commercial investment houses. Fees vary from program to program—although some programs have chosen not to charge fees in this highly competitive market, others charge a variety of fees (some obvious, others not so obvious). Look carefully at each plan's fee structure. As a tool to help review 529 plan options, including some basic questions to consider, reference the 529 Checklist in the appendix.

A couple of other good sources provide a broader review of the topic of saving and investments. One is The Investment Company Institute, which offers information on the mutual fund industry, at www.ici.org. Another organization that dedicates itself to investor protection issues is the North American Securities Administrators Association (NASAA) at www.nasaa.org.

529s and Their Impact on Financial Aid

529 plans were initially thought to be good investments only for those unlikely to qualify for need-based aid. This advice was based on the manner in which both federal and traditional institutional need-analysis methodologies treat 529 funds as investments at the point of withdrawal. As noted in chapter five's description of need-analysis methodologies, both the federal and institutional need-analysis formulas consider assets when determining what parents can pay annually toward their child's cost of attendance. Because parents have other responsibilities, including planning for retirement, these formulas assess parental assets at a lower rate, roughly 5 percent to 6 percent or less, than the assessment for student assets and income. That's appropriate; a

family's assets reflect their financial strength and should be considered as either the parent's or student's property.

The U.S. Department of Education, in a January 2004 document posted on the Information for Financial Aid Professionals online library, say the following about 529 programs in the determination of federal financial aid eligibility:

> [529 College Savings Plans] can be regarded as assets of the parent if the parent is the owner of the account, rather than the student, and thereby displace a smaller amount of financial aid. Distributions from . . . 529 College Savings Plans that are not subject to federal income tax are not counted as parent or student income in the determination of federal financial aid eligibility. Distributions for qualified educational expenses therefore do not reduce financial aid eligibility. The value of a 529 Prepaid Tuition Plan is not counted as an asset of either the owner or the beneficiary. Distributions are applied to the beneficiary's higher education expenses and reduce the cost of attendance. Distributions from 529 Prepaid Tuition Plans are not counted as parent or student income in the determination of financial aid. ("Treatment of Coverdell Accounts and 529 Tuition Plans," U.S. Department of Education, January 2004)

A MOVE TO COMMON SENSE

Although potential 529 investors should continue to be cautious, consider two points. First, in the late 1990s, the presidents at some thirty or so private colleges and universities, working with their financial aid officers, developed a new consensus need-analysis institutional methodology intended to generate more consistent results among participating institutions. These discussions have been conducted under the authority granted through another federal law (the Helping America's Children Act) and one of its provisions known as Section 568. Implemented in 2003 at participating institutions, this new 568 Consensus Approach to Need Analysis considers 529 funds established by parents to be the parent's assets. Withdrawals used to pay college expenses are viewed as the natural result of one's college savings plan (imagine that) and are, therefore, treated no differently than any other assets the parent may cash in and use to pay for college expenses. It is important to note that the 568 Consensus Approach only applies to the institutional methodology of determining financial aid eligibility; it does *not* apply to the federal methodology.

Second, there is at least some chance that the federal treatment of 529 plan assets and withdrawals will change in ways that encourage all investors to save for college expenses. To that end, there are several lobbying efforts currently underway. If this does happen, it is reasonable to assume that many, if not all, institutions will adopt a similar approach to the 568 Consensus Approach so that all such parent assets in the student's name will be treated more reasonably.

Except Washington, every state in the nation and the District of Columbia offers a 529 College Savings Plan. At the time this book was being written, twenty states (including Washington) also offered 529 Prepaid Tuition Plans.

Prepaid tuition certificates are a reasonably low-risk investment, and they are safe and affordable for most families. Although prepaid tuition certificates can often be used to finance attendance at in-state private as well as out-of-state institutions, the return on investment might be restricted if the fund is used to support private or out-of-state public institution expenses. Because such restrictions limit a student's enrollment options, read the fine print carefully.

College- and University-Sponsored Savings Plans

Originally developed as separate and unique to their individual institutions by a few individual private schools, these institution-specific plans have fallen out of favor in recent years because they required that the beneficiary attend the school that originated the fund, regardless of the student's particular interests and goals. Institutions also became a bit leery of these programs because participants expected their children to be offered admission, regardless of their abilities (or lack thereof).

Nonetheless, private institutions have, over time, become increasingly concerned about college affordability. Although every state has now developed a 529 program, these programs, as noted earlier, often involve restrictions such as limiting students to attend school in-state or forfeit some or all of the benefits that served as savings incentives for state residents. Institutions, particularly those in the private sector, were supportive of the new 529 plans but were also understandably concerned about the restrictions on these savings. To deal with this issue, eighteen southern colleges banded together in 1998 to found Tuition Plan, Inc. (www.tuitionplan.org or www.independent529plan.com). This 529 program (that covers only tuition and fees), later called Tuition Plan Consortium, has now expanded to more than 200 colleges and universities nationwide. Although it continues to attract mostly private institutions, the Consortium's membership has now expanded to include both large and small institutions nationwide and many Ivy League schools.

Tuition Plan Consortium, sponsors of the product known as Independent 529 Plan, rolled out its prepaid tuition program in fall 2003. Through an agreement with participating independent institutions, the Independent 529 Plan offers discounted tuition certificates to parents, grandparents, and other interested parties. These tuition certificates function essentially as cash—they can be used to pay a fixed percentage of tuition at any participating institution. The good news—in addition to a guarantee of tuition as provided through the 529 prepaid-tuition provision—is the discount Independent 529 institutions offer to purchasers. Each participating independent institution establishes a discount rate annually. This pre-established discount rate applies to the certificate until it is cashed in. The percentage of tuition each certificate pays at redemption depends on each school's annual price of attendance at the time the certificate is presented, the same as provided through any other 529 Prepaid Tuition Plan. Proceeds from initial certificate sales are invested by Tuition Plan Consortium with TIAA-CREF, a highly respected national financial institution that specializes in college-related financial services. When a certificate is presented, the recipient institution provides the presenter with the percentage of tuition promised at the time of purchase. The institution, in turn, presents the tuition certificate to the Tuition Plan Consortium bank and is paid the original value of the investment plus any earnings accrued during the period in which it has been held by TIAA-CREF. Purchasers of certificates are guaranteed the percentage of tuition established by each participating institution. Some investment risk (and potential reward) is transferred from the purchasers to the colleges in exchange for the assurance that part or all of their college tuition is covered.

So Which Program Is Best?

A wide range of options are available for families interested in saving for college, and you need to figure out what works best for you. Remember, some of these plans offer special tax considerations, while others offer fund growth incentives or purchase incentives. Some are limited in various ways, while others are less restrictive.

Choosing what program works best for you and/or for the beneficiary is a pretty personal matter: The best plan for one family may not be the best one for another. A prepaid tuition program does provide a guarantee and a modicum of comfort in the sense that regardless of future increases in tuition, the program will honor whatever percentage of tuition it was at the time of purchase. State programs may provide additional state tax considerations. The Independent 529 Plan or Tuition Plan Consortium offers similar guarantees and a discount but not the state tax break. If you are thinking about the 529 plan approach and are comparing it to college savings programs offered by private investment companies—which might offer greater returns—keep in mind that your state's saving program may provide state income tax breaks as well as the opportunity to buy shares in the state 529 plan (either with modest annual management fees or possibly less expensive fees than those charged commercially). Also noteworthy, especially for some state 529 Prepaid Tuition Plans, is the fact that many of them include a time limit—for example, ten years from date of college entrance or the beneficiary reaching a certain age—by which time the program must be used.

On each program's website (see the appendix), take the time to compare the various provisions available. As the concept has gained momentum, changes continue to take place, many of which make such 529 programs even more attractive to purchasers. These changes include larger maximums, more portability, revised restrictions on the opportunity to purchase additional units, and even opportunities for purchase by out-of-state individuals.

THE END IS NIGH?

By the way, the TRA '97 has a provision which would terminate the favorable tax considerations at the end of the year 2010. So officially, these wonderful tax benefits are scheduled to cease on January 1, 2011.

The common opinion right now, however, is that this so-called "sunset" provision will more than likely be revised by congress, effectively either extending these benefits beyond 2010 or possibly even making the benefits a permanent part of the tax code. So far, 529 programs certainly seem to be serving their purpose—which was to encourage the planning and saving for college—since billions of dollars have already been invested nationally.

CHAPTER EIGHT: OKAY, SO WE DIDN'T SAVE ENOUGH. NOW WHAT?

THE GOOD NEWS

Finally, the day arrives. A thick letter arrives from the admissions office and your child tears it open quickly (thick envelopes generally contain good news). In euphoria, you call the aunts, uncles, cousins, and next-door neighbors to tell them the good news, and your son or daughter sends the college a letter back, accepting its offer. You're justifiably proud of your student—and then reality sets in.

You need to pay for this piece of good news. Your children did their part, and now it's up to you.

In the best of all possible scenarios, that letter of acceptance came with a financial aid award letter. Your family contribution seems reasonable, and the award meets full need. Perhaps your children even earned a merit scholarship. Thankfully, you saved for your children's college education. The savings won't cover the entire cost of attendance, but by regularly allocating some of your monthly income to your college savings account and by having your children also save a reasonable amount of their college costs (and continuing to do so in college), these resources, along with those detailed on the award letter, will work. While it won't be easy, it is doable.

Ouch!

But what if the financial aid award *doesn't* fill the gap between the cost of attendance and the amount you can make available each month from savings, your current income, and your children's contributions? How do you bridge this gap? And what if the answer to your request for financial aid is a resounding "Sorry, but you don't qualify for any form of assistance"?

First, try to understand the nature of the financial aid office's answer. Did you qualify for less aid than you realistically expected? If so, sit down and draft a letter to the aid office providing dollar-specific details regarding any extenuating circumstances that reduce your family's ability to support educational expenses. Determining need or aid eligibility is a relative science; that is, families with similar circumstances are treated in similar ways, while families with proportionally different circumstances are treated in proportionally different ways. Your job is to provide the aid office with the kind of information that leads it to consider an exception to the consistently applied, formula-driven answer your aid request initially received.

Remember, while your circumstances are understandable to you, it's less easy for the complete stranger in the financial aid office. Think about the nondiscretionary circumstances that reduce your financial strength. Don't dwell on cost-of-living, credit card debt, car payments, and the like. Virtually everyone has these or similar expenses, so they don't do much to set you apart from other families requesting financial aid. Generally speaking, financial aid offices aren't willing to consider discretionary circumstances or debts. Detail the legal, uninsured medical, business, and prior educational debt you are now coping with. Explain the reason for the debt, the total due, and the monthly hit on your finances. Perhaps you have ongoing, non-reimbursed medical expenses or special educational costs for a younger child, or maybe you are paying some or all of the expenses associated with a parent's stay in a nursing home. These are the circumstances that can lead the aid office to reevaluate your children's aid eligibility. Be sure to provide details—more information is always better than less information—and be prepared to fully document your circumstances. Remember the primary guideline: Any special circumstances you plan to use as the basis of your appeal should relate to unusual, nondiscretionary expenses.

If you still need help beyond that made available through the aid office, you will typically have several months in which to reduce or close the gap between cost and available resources. Although the savings you accumulate in this period aren't likely to eliminate your problem, these resources can help reduce the funding gap. Do what you can, regardless of how much time you have left. And don't forget the extended family. Grandparents can sometimes help find ways to help close the college affordability gap, so don't be shy.

PLAN B

If you have counted all possible savings and exhausted all opportunities for additional financial aid, it's time to turn to loans. A variety of reasonable options are available. Unless your children have already somehow incurred serious credit problems, virtually all students eligible for some amount of federal financial aid can borrow from the Stafford Student Loan Program; many will qualify for a federal subsidy covering interest expenses while they are enrolled. The interest rates charged after graduation or for those who do not qualify for the interest subsidy, while the student is in school (and are typically extremely reasonable and in the recent past have been remarkably low). Interest is subject to change annually on July 1 and is capped at 8.25 percent and floats under that. This interest rate is set using T-bill rates plus an index. In the period from 2003 to 2004, the rate was set at an amazingly low 3.2 percent. Currently, students can borrow $2,625 in the first year of enrollment, $3,500 in the second year, and $5,500 in the third and fourth years (additional funding is available for student enrolling in graduate or professional programs). Although the lending provisions are basically similar, some institutions will typically direct you to one of several preferred lenders (participating banks, credit unions, or other lending organizations), or to the "Direct Loan" program through which the school directly provides the student loan. Sometimes local organizations provide private loan funds at low interest rates. Check with your church or local civic organization and with your high school guidance counselor.

If a student loan doesn't fill the gap, a number of financing opportunities are currently available for parents. Many of these loans allow some or all principle payments to be deferred and interest payment charges to be capitalized and repaid following the completion of school. However, before you turn to a federal or even a commercial parent loan program, you may want to consider a home equity loan. If you have accumulated a significant amount of equity, the value of this asset you own may provide a source of reasonably cheap financing. Interest is usually deductible on your federal tax forms and, most importantly, the borrower often has a great deal of flexibility with respect to the repayment period. We talked earlier about paying after your children attend college—both parent and home equity loans provide just this opportunity.

One of the authors used the same home equity money over and over while his children were in college. (Talk to your financial advisor before doing this; they might not recommend it if you're close to retirement.) At the beginning of each academic year, he borrowed enough from home equity to fill the yawning gap between the cost of attendance and the family's then-available resources. The family then spent the next twelve months repaying as much of that debt as possible. At the beginning of the next academic year, the family borrowed the amount they'd repaid plus enough to close that particular year's financing gap, and then repeated this through eight consecutive years of college expenses for two children. Although the educational debt grew each year, the family managed to keep it under control by focusing on repaying as much as possible as the school year progressed—reasoning that it would be easier to repay this debt after graduation, after biannual tuition bills. And it worked exactly as planned.

If a home equity loan doesn't work for your family, consider one of a burgeoning number of parent-loans programs designed to support educational expenses. These loans are similar in four essential ways.

- Annual interest rates are almost always lower than those charged for commercial bank loans.

- All such plans feature extended payment plans, some for as long as twenty-five years.

- Creditworthy parents can borrow up to as much as the difference between the cost of attendance and available financial aid.

- Some of the interest on these loans may be tax deductible.

The most popular parent loan is the PLUS Loan—Parent Loan to Undergraduate Students. Offered by state agencies and local and national banks, this federally insured loan program allows parents with good recent credit histories to repay these loans over a ten-year period. Interest is capped at 9 percent annually and floats under that, based on a T-bill rate plus an index as set on July 1. The credit requirements are less stringent, so start here if credit is likely to be a problem for your family. If you do have credit problems, some of the national educational lenders will try to work with families to help repair credit ratings. Sometimes making the financial aid office aware of your credit problems (details are important here) might help with your loan application and, possibly, your application for institutional assistance. It doesn't work for every family, but it is worth considering.

Commercial parent loans for education typically carry higher rates than those offered by the PLUS program, though these nongovernment educational loan options generally have lower interest rates than those associated with regular bank loans. Repayment on these loans can often be extended for as long as twenty-five years. Interest rates and repayment terms vary considerably, so shop around before your commit to a particular lender. The Internet is a great place to begin shopping (again, check the appendix). In some of these nongovernment education loan programs, the loan must be taken out in the student's name, but the signature of a credit-worthy person, such as the student's parent, is required. In many cases where a cosigner is required, some lenders will agree to release the cosigner from repayment responsibility once the borrower has made a specified number of on-time repayments (for example, forty-eight months).

Having presented these additional sources for borrowing, we need to stress that it's extremely important to retain money for emergency reserve. While you might consider borrowing through certain forms of life insurance—and while that might be possible—it wouldn't leave you with emergency money in reserve. And if you're putting your children through college, it's always a good idea to have a little extra money, left untouched, in reserve.

Finally, some parents might be tempted to consider turning to retirement plans for educational financing. That's about the worst thing in the world a parent approaching retirement could do. Such borrowing might not only put a severe amount of pressure on a parent's retirement plans, but also produce penalties and taxes that can often make this approach prohibitively expensive. There would be many factors to consider, including the value of this asset, your age at the time, the length of time remaining prior to your planned retirement, and other obligations regarding this asset. Consider such financing plans only as a last resort, unless your available resources allow you to finance your child's education and still retire at a reasonable age.

Chapter Nine: How to Help Your Student Cut Costs and Contribute

Good Old-Fashioned Common Sense

Earlier in this book, we suggested that students aren't likely to be able to significantly reduce their costs of attendance. Although this is true in most cases, a variety of savings opportunities are available for the cost-conscious student. As you would expect, these cost-reduction opportunities are, for the most part, related to the student's lifestyle and personal choices.

Encourage them to be realistic about expenses and to remember that they are on a tight budget. Review carefully with them how much money will be available to them for the coming year's miscellaneous expenses after paying for tuition, fees, and room and board, and consider drawing up a monthly budget to help them plan their expenditures. One of the reasons they're in school is to enhance their earning power in ways that will make a variety of pleasures affordable, but only after graduation. Your son or daughter does not want to find that college expenses that they could have avoided have made their post-graduation life difficult.

Credit Cards

If you decide that your children should have a credit card for emergencies (and only emergencies), use a card that requires that the entire balance be paid at the end of the month, such as

American Express: This option can often eliminate or reduce interest charges. By paying their bill at the end of each month students can avoid excessive credit card debts that, over time, make it difficult for them to remain in school—and that can ruin their credit rating in the process. These credit problems could get even messier when such credit card debts are combined with excessive student loan indebtedness. This dire combination will have major lifelong consequences with which no one would want to be burdened, especially if they could have been avoided with some good old-fashioned common sense: If you don't have the money, don't spend it!

One credit card should be sufficient. A credit card, if used wisely and responsibly (and again, only for emergencies), can be a reasonable resource. They can help to build a young person's credit ratings in ways that will support their future aspirations and dreams for major financing needs, including a home and a car. The irresponsible use of credit cards, however, can lead to financial disaster.

All of us want our children to make wise choices early in their lives to help ensure a solid platform for bigger goals later in life. The earlier they can learn budget-building, responsible credit card use, and ways to safeguard their personal finances from credit card and personal identification fraud, the better off they will be when they are older.

Some Cost-Cutting Ideas

So how does a student reduce the cost of attendance? Here are a number of ways.

Room and board expenses: Room costs often vary considerably. While some institutions do not ask incoming students what kind of room they want, almost all will be willing to have a student request a different room, particularly if they are assigned a single or inordinately expensive room. Don't be shy about asking for a different room assignment. Junior and senior students are almost always given some level of room choice. At the very least, unless your student has some special needs, avoid single rooms. They not only tend to isolate a student, but also cost a lot more than double rooms.

Students often move off campus to save money. While it is possible to save money by renting an apartment or house with friends and roommates, plenty of expenses are included in the college's room-and-board cost, which aren't included in renting: gas, water, electricity, phone/Internet, cable expenses, and renters' insurance all add up. Preparing food costs money and time as well—and some institutions may require even off-campus student to eat some or all of their meals on campus.

Then there's transportation. If the move is within walking or biking distance of campus, that's great; transportation costs can be managed. If not, consider the cost of bus fares (forget about cabs; they're too expensive to take every day). A motorcycle probably isn't a good idea—they're dangerous and the insurance is expensive. Used cars can end up being expensive to maintain. New cars are so expensive as to make moving off campus to save money ridiculous. And with any car, there are insurance, gas and oil, license fees, tires, maintenance and repair, and campus-parking charges.

Consider all of the possibilities, budget for the unexpected, and factor in the "cost" of inconvenience—looking for parking, time spent getting back and forth to campus, the sometimes long break between classes that might strand a noncampus resident on campus. Living off campus can be enjoyable, but it can make living within a tight budget difficult.

Books and supplies: Now here is a place students can often save a bit of money. The average cost of books alone is estimated to be $750 to $850 per year. For some majors, books can be even more expensive. Consider buying used books—they are far less expensive than new books. You will find that this is particularly true at off campus bookstores. They do a volume business with students and can often provide real savings opportunities. Similarly, less expensive options for purchasing the very same textbooks can sometimes be found by shopping online.

Your student may not need to hang on to books unless they are particularly important or they relate to their major. Attics around the country are full of books parents saved from college, and eventually, they end up in the book section of their church's fall rummage sale or on the trash pile. Selling used books will help pay for new books each semester. So get rid of at least some of them—unless, of course, your house has a particularly large attic or you expect to be a major player at your church's annual bazaar.

Computers: Computers are pretty much a necessity at college, though it doesn't necessarily follow that your student must have a new, top-of-the-line laptop. Some college campuses require students to own computers; if this is the case, this expense will almost always be included in the cost-of-attendance budget. Most institutions, however, provide computer labs in a variety of locations around campus. These locations offer computers, printers, Web access, and a great deal of software that your student can use free.

Always check with your student's school before you purchase a computer. Many schools have been able to arrange for bulk purchase of computers, resulting in significantly reduced prices for students. You may also discover that some institutions prefer their students to have a certain kind of computer. If you must buy a new one, remember that the computer will likely be mid-grade technology before your student graduates, so think twice before shelling out big bucks for all the bells and whistles.

Personal Expenses: Of the many expenses students confront in college, personal expenses represent the most easily controlled aspect of the budget. Personal expenses, although easy to control, are difficult to resist. Clothing is a great example: While college students do need nice clothing for special occasions, day-in, day-out campus garb is, at best, very casual. At the risk of being obvious, purchases made at factory outlets, sales racks, used or vintage shops, and discount basements can be made frugally. Don't forget irregular items (your student will be the only one to know), samples, and manufacturer's closeouts.

Campus entertainment: Most institutions offer a variety of inexpensive campus activities. These include concerts, student produced plays, basketball, football, and other sports events. Broadway plays are often staged on campus, some as they tune up for their New York opening. There is almost always a wonderful array of campus speakers appearing throughout the academic year. These are not only free or inexpensive but also intellectually stimulating and academically helpful. And speaking of intellectually stimulating, there are museums and art galleries on or near most college campuses. Movies shown on campus are often between their initial theater run and the video store and are far cheaper than they would be in the theater. You may have to bring your own popcorn—but campus movies make for a cheap date.

If all else fails, there are always campus parties thrown by various social groups, living groups, fraternities, sororities, and clubs. Legitimate concerns about campus alcohol consumption and, in some cases, alcohol abuse have reduced the number and level of parties given at many institutions, but there is still plenty of activity. You will, of course, want to caution your student about alcohol consumption; a thoughtful and responsible student, well-armed with the facts, will be fine.

Communication: Students can write or e-mail instead of calling—correspondence is cheaper that way (stamps cost next to nothing and e-mail is usually free at school). When it comes to cell phones, recommend that your children not take one to school unless they can adhere to a cheap plan. Many cell phone plans offer unlimited long distance and free minutes; while convenient for keeping in touch, usage outside of these free times can get pricey and it adds up.

For all of these personal, incidental, and social expenses, you and your children should establish a monthly miscellaneous allowance as a simple means of budgeting and controlling costs. This practice will allow students to accept full responsibility for managing their personal expenses.

Transportation: Some institutions prohibit students, particularly freshmen, from bringing vehicles to campus. And for institutions that do allow cars, parking can be a problem. Many campuses offer extensive and often free bus transportation to boot, so getting around shouldn't be a problem. If your children do take cars to campus, consider what we mentioned earlier; having a car on campus will probably be prohibitively expensive, regardless of those cost-saving techniques you establish.

Most campuses sponsor ride boards where students with cars can advertise rides to a particular place in exchange for a little gas money. Likewise, students without cars can put up notices asking for a ride to, say, New Orleans on or about December 15 with a return to campus on or about January 10. These ride boards work well and can help students reduce their transportation costs. In a few institutions, there may also be alumni organizations that will help organize transportation to their alma mater. This could be particularly helpful at the beginning and ending of the school year, when some alumni clubs help to organize rental trucks for moving the big stuff that may not fit in a car, train, bus, or plane.

If your student can't find a ride, there is always the bus or train. These both offer economical transportation. If flying is necessary, book flights early enough to take advantage of cheaper rates; early planning can make a huge difference in ticket prices. If they are traveling during peak travel times, suggest that they get to the airport early and put their names on their airline's "bump" list. If they get bumped from the scheduled flight, the airline will provide them with a free ticket or certificate for ticket purchases at a later date. If they have to spend the night near the airport, airlines will often pay their expenses. They may get home a bit later than planned, but doing so could help pay for their next trip. That's a worthwhile trade-off.

BUDGETING

There are, of course, other ways for you and your student to save money at college. Your home grocery bill will certainly drop, so keep that in mind. Careful and thoughtful budgeting is key; you can use a budget guide similar to the following to plan your expenses.

Available Resources

- Parent Contribution   _____
- Student Contribution from Savings _____
- Financial Aid   _____
- Summer and Campus Earnings   _____
- Other Resources   _____
- Total Available Resources   _____

Expenses

- Tuition and Fees   _____
- Books and Supplies   _____
- Room   _____
- Board   _____
- Transportation   _____
- Personal Expenses (list as appropriate)

_____   _____

_____   _____

_____   _____

_____   _____

Total Expenses   _____

The budgeting process will initially be a trial-and-error effort. Keeping track of expenses will make a difference—it will not only help the planning process for the following year, but also encourage your student to think carefully about any expenses they are considering.

ONE MORE ISSUE ON COST REDUCTION

Just as the growing cost of a college education is a legitimate concern for most families, so is the issue of students who don't complete their undergraduate degree within the standard four-year period. We don't mean those special programs that may formally require a fifth year, like programs in architecture; nor are we referring to individuals enrolled in cooperative education programs in which students are employed full-time (in an internship capacity) for one or more academic terms as a formal part of their educational experience. The problem comes with students who take less than a full load of courses or repeatedly change their majors to the point at which they'll be enrolled for five, six, seven, or more years. This extended period of enrollment has a huge and negative impact on families as well as institutions, public policymakers, federal and state governments, and, of course, taxpayers. Certainly the college years are the best years of your life, but it is important for students to graduate as soon as possible.

Why is this a cost issue? First of all, there is the obvious extra cost incurred by the student and family for the additional academic term(s) needed to complete the degree. In too many cases, this may include additional educational debt assumed by the student and/or parents. Equally important and expensive is the cost of "lost opportunity;" that is, the student's loss of wages they would have been earning, had they graduated on schedule and actually gotten a job (that is, after all, one goal of college).

Then there's the cost to the institution for the additional educational services required for these students to complete their programs. Instructors have to be paid, classrooms and other facilities maintained, utilities must be paid for, and counseling provided. The longer students are enrolled, the more expensive they become.

If the student is receiving any form of student financial aid, whether from public or private sources, this too could have been provided to another student. If the individual is enrolled in the public sector, where every enrolled student's instructional costs are heavily subsidized by taxpayer funds, cost also becomes a significant, albeit less noticeable issue.

Finally, another cost is borne by those prospective students whose spaces in the institution are filled by students still enrolled beyond the standard four-year program. These individuals, in a very real sense, also pay since they are not allowed to enroll because of limitations on enrollment. The cost of lost opportunity is a hidden but real expense for these students.

Again, while some of the reasons for these problems may be understandable and unavoidable, smart consumers would be wise to ask admissions officers what the institution's on-time, (in four years) graduation rate is—and if this number is low, why? What is the institution's retention rate from freshman to sophomore year? Are enough courses available each semester so that students who carefully plan their academic program can expect to receive their degree on time? If classes are available and students are still not graduating on time, is the academic counseling not available? If a student drops a course, is this done for good reason, with appropriate academic counseling and with a plan to make it up in the summer or with an additional course load the following semester?

You may want to ask currently enrolled students (especially those pursuing a curriculum which may be of interest to your student) some of these questions. College is expensive enough without having to add unnecessarily to the already significant cost, so check into these matters when you research possible colleges. You may also want to have a heart-to-heart conversation with your son or daughter about the responsibility they must accept for ensuring a proper course load to finish on time.

Finally, some students through no fault of their own may have to stop out for one or more terms due to unexpected family emergencies or serious financial setbacks. Such circumstances have and always will serve to extend graduation dates. Short of this kind of easily understandable circumstance, you should expect your child to complete their undergraduate degree in four or fewer years.

GETTING THE RIGHT INFO

One more point is worthwhile mentioning: A recent NCES study and similar surveys of parents with high school-age students have consistently concluded that many parents significantly overestimate the costs of both public and private college. Many reasons may help to explain such poor information—

some understandable; others, perhaps less so. But the bottom line is that the age-old problem of getting the right information out there at the critical time will probably always be with us, and it's up to you to seek out good, accurate, timely information far in advance of the college days.

CHAPTER 10: OUR FINAL THOUGHTS

Our Final Thoughts

Although paying for college won't ever be easy, the material provided here, especially that related to planning and saving, should serve to help make the process more manageable.

Remember the following:

- Paying for college is hard.

- Create a specific strategy that allows you to pay before, during, and after enrollment.

- Involve the entire family—make paying for college a team project.

- Give your children specific paying-for-college goals. After all, they are the ones who will enjoy the benefits of a college education.

- Make your paying-for-college plan an integral part of your family's overall finances.

- Make paying for college as automatic as possible.

- Start early; saved money is cheaper than borrowed money.

- Remember, the sooner you start, the more help compounding interest will provide.

- Be realistic about the costs of attendance.

- Help your children to be realistic about the costs of attendance and to control their expenses.

- At the point of enrollment, consider all the possible paying-for-college options and remember that there are many options available to each family.

- Apply for need-based aid at least once, regardless of your circumstances.

- Make certain that the student-aid office understands any circumstances that affect your family's ability to support educational expenses.

- Remember that paying over time, carefully managed, increases your college-purchasing power.

- Insist that your student be responsible about student-loan debt and borrow no more than is absolutely necessary.

- Remember that paying for college is an investment and that the increase in lifetime earnings will substantially exceed the costs of attendance.

The day your child departs for college is a very special moment for every family. In many ways, the departure date, bittersweet as it might be, marks the culmination of years of hard work and planning and, more importantly, it represents the achievement of many of the dreams and aspirations that you, as a parent, have invested in your child. Although paying for college is expensive and requires sacrifice, think of it as the final gift (or expense) associated with raising your child. Given the ever-increasing need for higher education and the rather extraordinary lifelong benefits associated with obtaining a college degree, you may even want to consider the gift of paying for college as your legacy.

Remember to do all you can to ensure that your son or daughter has the educational opportunities that allow them to be all that they can be. This is one of the greatest gifts you could ever give them.

GLOSSARY

568 President's Group—A group of mostly private-school presidents who believed that need-based aid continues to be the most appropriate manner in which to distribute institutional financial aid resources. This group developed the Consensus Approach to Need Analysis.

AGI—Adjusted Gross Income of the amount listed on line 34 of the IRS 1040 form.

Alternative or Commercial Loans—Banks, some state agencies, and some educational institutions offer loans through which creditworthy parents may borrow up to the annual cost of education less any financial aid their student receives.

Award Letter—A letter from a college or university that details the amount and type of aid that will be available to the student.

College Board—The oldest educational organization in the United States that works to support students as they make the transition from secondary school to college.

College Scholarship Service (CSS)—As the financial aid arm of The College Board, CSS sponsors the PROFILE.

CollegeSure CD Program—This private savings plan offers federally insured certificates of deposit indexed to the growth of tuition in a select group of national institutions.

Consensus Approach to Need Analysis—Developed by a group of approximately thirty institutions, the Consensus Approach is designed to return consistency to the determination of parent ability to pay. Also known as the 568 Consensus Approach.

Cost of Attendance—Student cost-of-attendance budgets generally include tuition and fees, room, board, books, miscellaneous expenses, and travel.

Coverdell IRAs—These educational IRAs are essentially trust accounts specifically designed to pay the educational expenses of a designated beneficiary.

Custodial Accounts—The Uniform Gift to Minors Act or Uniform Transfers to Minors Act allows savings accounts to be opened under a minor's name while allowing the investor to retain control of the account.

Education Bonds—Series EE purchased after January 1990 and Series I bonds provide long-term tax-free savings opportunities. The tax-free benefits phase out as income increases.

Expected Family Contribution (EFC)—Families submitting the Free Application for Federal Student Aid will receive a Student Aid Report from the Department of Education. The EFC is the family contribution used to determine eligibility for federal student aid.

FAFSA—All applicants for federal Title IV resources must complete this document and submit it directly to the Department of Education. These forms will be processed and distributed to all institutions listed by the applicant.

Federal Methodology (FM)—A streamlined need-analysis methodology for determining eligibility for federal Title IV student aid. FM was designed by Congress and is updated periodically by the Department of Education.

Federal Perkins Loan—A low interest (5 percent), deferred-payment federal loan. Interest is subsidized while the student remains in school.

Financial Aid Package—When meeting a student's need, institutions "package" student aid, which could include different amounts of campus employment, student loans, grants, and/or scholarships.

Financial Need—If the family contribution is less than the cost of attendance, the student is said to have demonstrated financial need.

Grant Funds—Provided by a variety of sources, including federal and state governments, private organizations, and colleges and universities, these are essentially free funds that do not have to be earned or repaid.

Hope Scholarship Program—Authorized by Congress, the Hope Scholarship provides tax credits for individuals paying for tuition and fees paid during the tax year. The maximum credit is $1,500.

Independent 529 Program—Also know as the Tuition Plan, Inc., this prepaid college savings program offers discounted tuition certificates. More than 225 private institutions participate in this national college savings program.

Institutional Aid Applications—Some colleges and universities require an institutionally developed aid application designed to further supplement standard national forms such as the FAFSA and the PROFILE.

Institutional Methodology—The traditional need-analysis methodology, developed by the educational community, is generally used to determine eligibility for institutional or private funds.

Lifetime Learning Credit—Individuals paying tuition and fees for post-secondary qualified studies after the first and second year of college. Eligible taxpayers may claim a $1,000 tax credit.

Local or Outside Scholarships—Scholarships available in the local community are sometimes provided by churches or synagogues, civic organizations, local businesses, employers, and national associations.

MAGI—Modified Adjusted Gross Income

Merit Scholarships—Institutional grants offered to students because of special academic achievement or special talent in art, music, or some other area.

Need-analysis—The process through the Department of Education or a college or university that determines eligibility for need-based aid.

Need-blind Admission—Institutions that admit students without considering their eligibility for financial aid.

Parent Contribution—The need-analysis-determined amount the parent(s) are expected to contribute toward their child's annual cost of attendance.

Parent Loan to Undergraduate Students (PLUS)—Parents of undergraduate students without recent credit problems may borrow the annual cost of attendance less any financial aid their children are receiving. Repayment begins six weeks after funds are disbursed.

Pell Grants—Federal grants made available to low income students as annually determined by filing the FAFSA.

PROFILE—The aid application generally required for institutional or private student aid resources. Forms will be processed and distributed to all institutions listed by the applicant.

ROTC Programs—Reserve Officer Training Corps programs are sponsored by the air force, army, navy, and Marine Corps. Participants receive grants to cover some or all tuition, fees, and a monthly stipend. Participants are generally required to spend some time on activity duty.

Roth IRA—This alternative to a regular IRA allows the funds to be used for retirement as well as other savings goals to include higher education.

Scholarship Search Companies—Many companies offer to help students locate scholarship support, generally for a fee. Information on virtually any scholarship support for which a student might be eligible is available free and can be located through research in the local library or a student's guidance counselor's office.

Self Help—The portion of a need-based aid award generally made up of campus employment and student loans.

SEOG Grants—Federal grants awarded by institutions to low income students as determined by the FAFSA.

Stafford Student Loans (Subsidized)—Students who demonstrate need by filing the FAFSA may borrow interest-free Stafford funds. Student may borrow $2,500 as freshmen, $3,500 as sophomores, and $5,500 as juniors and seniors and fifth-year undergraduates up to a total limit of $23,000. Borrowers have up to ten years, beginning six months after graduation, to repay their loans

Stafford Student Loans (Unsubsidized)—Students who fail to qualify for the interest subsidy may borrow, without benefit of the interest subsidy, from the Stafford Loan Program. Other aspects of the program are the same, regardless of a borrower's eligibility for the interest subsidy.

Student Contribution—The family contribution generally includes a student's expectation based on consideration of the student's assets and any continuing income the student may receive. This expectation almost always includes a summer saving expectation that requires a student to work during the summer and use some of the earnings to support educational expenses during the following academic year.

Summer Earnings Expectation—Student aid packages generally include an expectation that the student will get a summer job and save a portion of their earnings to help pay for costs of attendance in the upcoming academic year. Expectations differ significantly from institution to institution.

Taxpayer Relief Act of 1997—Congress passed this act that, among other provisions, authorizes 529 Savings Accounts.

TIAA-CREF—A private investment firm that specializes in fund management, generally in the educational arena.

APPENDIX

APPENDIX A: REVIEW OF 529 PROGRAMS

All 50 states and the District of Columbia now participate in a 529 program. Some offer the prepaid tuition plan, some offer the college savings plan, and some offer both. States that provide both programs may allow you to participate in both for the same beneficiary. In addition, a new and different 529 program was announced in September 2003 that currently involves more than 225 private institutions nationally. While none of these programs provide a guarantee of admission for an individual beneficiary, the wide range of post-secondary education opportunities available for using the benefits of a 529 program will surely provide virtually all beneficiaries with choices. In some state programs, there will be variations of 529 programs made available through financial advisors. Adding to the flexibility of these programs is that one 529 program can be rolled over to another.

The information in this section of the book attempts to offer a snapshot view of each of these 529 programs. They are listed in alphabetical order, with the private 529 program, officially sponsored by the Tuition Plan Consortium and known as the Independent 529 Plan, listed at the end. Although not always the policy from the beginning, 529 plans have increasingly become more portable to out-of-state institutions, as long as the school is considered eligible for participation for federal student aid by the federal government. Of course, the Independent 529 is a totally portable program to any of the participating institutions and may be secured without state residency limitations.

In each snapshot, there will be a reference to the program's website and to other sources from which more detailed and more current information can be obtained. In addition to those listed below, many states offer additional options sold through a financial advisor or broker. Look further into these resources, especially since provisions for some of them may have changed.

Alabama Prepaid Affordable Tuition (PACT)
Type: prepaid
Phone: 800-252-7228
Website: www.treasury.state.al.us
Eligibility: no residency requirement; 9th grade or below
State tax: favorable at distribution
Minimum/Maximum: yes; amount based on age of recipient
Fees: $75 upon enrollment
Management: State Board of Trustees
Other: tuition packages and payment options available

Alabama Higher Education 529 Fund (HE 529 Fund)
Type: college savings
Phone: 866-529-2228
Website: www.treasury.state.al.us
Eligibility: in-state residency at time of enrollment
State tax: no favorable consideration
Minimum/Maximum: yes, per portfolio: $250 min.; $269,000 max.
Fees: annual $10 maintenance fee possible
Management: Van Kampen Asset Management, Inc.
Other: investment choices—three options

Alaska: University of Alaska College Savings Plan
Type: college savings
Phone: 866-277-1005
Website: www.uacollegesavings.com
Eligibility: no residency requirement or age requirement
State tax: N/A; Alaska has no state income tax

Minimum/Maximum: yes, per portfolio: $250 min.; $250,000 max. per beneficiary
Fees: not upon enrollment but annual $30 maintenance fee possible
Management: T. Rowe Price Associates, Inc.
Other: earnings guaranteed to keep pace with University of Alaska tuition

Arizona Family College Savings Program
Type: college savings
Phone: 800-888-2723
Website: http://arizona@collegesavings.com
Eligibility: no residency or age requirement
State tax: favorable at distribution
Minimum/Maximum: $250 min.; $197,000 max. per beneficiary
Fees: none
Management: College Savings Bank
Other: limited investment options but rate of return adjusted based on national cost index

Arkansas Gift College Investing Plan
Type: college savings
Phone: 877-615-4116
Website: www.thegiftplan.com
Eligibility: must be state resident but no age requirement
State tax: favorable at distribution
Minimum/Maximum: $250 min.; $245,000 max. per beneficiary
Fees: none
Management: Mercury Advisors
Other: investment options available; no guarantee of return

California State Scholarship Trust
Type: college savings
Phone: 877-728-4338
Website: www.scholarshare.com
Eligibility: no residency or age requirements
State tax: favorable at distribution
Minimum/Maximum: $25 min.; $267,580 max. per beneficiary
Fees: no
Management: TIAA/CREF Tuition Financing, Inc.
Other: investment choices available based on age of beneficiary; provides guarantee of principal and a fixed rate of return

Colorado CollegeInvest—Scholars Choice College Savings Program
Type: college savings
Phone: 800-478-5651; 888-572-4652
Website: www.scholars-choice.com
Eligibility: no residency or age requirements
State tax: contributions deductible; favorable at distribution

Minimum/Maximum: $25 min.; $235,000 max. per beneficiary
Fees: no
Management: Citigroup Asset Management
Other: investment options available

Colorado Stable Value Plus College Savings Program
Type: college savings
Phone: 800-478-5651
Website: www.collegeinvest.org
Eligibility: no residency requirements or age requirements
State tax: contributions deductible; favorable at distribution
Minimum/Maximum: $25 min.; $235,000 max. per beneficiary
Fees: $20 application fee
Management: Travelers Insurance Company
Other: limited investment option based on annually determined interest rate

Connecticut Higher Education Trust (CHET)
Type: college savings
Phone: 888-799-2438
Website: www.aboutchet.com
Eligibility: no residency requirements or age requirements
State tax: favorable at distribution
Minimum/Maximum: $25 min.; $235,000 max. per beneficiary
Fees: no
Management: TIAA/CREF Tuition Financing, Inc.
Other: limited investment options

Delaware College Investment Plan
Type: college savings
Phone: 800-544-1655
Website: www.fidelity.com/delaware
Eligibility: no residency requirements or age requirements
State tax: favorable at distribution
Minimum/Maximum: $500 min.; $250,000 max. per beneficiary
Fees: annual maintenance $30 fee possible
Management: Fidelity Investments
Other: limited investment options

D.C. College Savings Plan (Washington, D.C.)
Type: college savings
Phone: 800-987-4859 (D.C. residents); 800-368-2745 (non residents)
Website: www.dccollegesavings.com
Eligibility: must be resident of the District of Columbia but no age requirements
State tax: Qualified deductions; favorable for District of Columbia residents at distribution
Minimum/Maximum: varies: $25 to $100 min.; $260,000 max. per beneficiary

Fees: no application fee but annual $15 maintenance fee
Management: Calvert Asset Management Co., Inc.
Other: investment options available

Florida Prepaid College Tuition Program

Type: prepaid tuition
Phone: 800-552-4723
Website: www.florida529plans.com
Eligibility: residency required for beneficiary at time of purchase
State tax: favorable for Florida intangibles tax; Florida has no state tax
Minimum/Maximum: $2,827 min.; $31,901 max.
Fees: $50 application fee
Management: Florida Prepaid College Board
Other: various tuition and payment options available

Florida College Investment Plan

Type: college savings
Phone: 800-552-4723
Website: www.florida529plans.com
Eligibility: no residency requirement; no age requirement
State tax: favorable for Florida intangibles tax; Florida has no state tax
Minimum/Maximum: $25 min.; $283,000 per beneficiary
Fees: $50 application fee
Management: Florida Prepaid College Board
Other: investment options available

Georgia Higher Education Savings Plan

Type: college savings
Phone: 877-424-4377
Website: www.gacollegesavings.com
Eligibility: no residency or age requirements
State tax: favorable
Minimum/Maximum: $25 min.; $235,000 per beneficiary
Fees: no
Management: TIAA/CREF Tuition Financing, Inc.
Other: investment options available

Hawaii Tuition EDGE Plan

Type: college savings
Phone: 866-529-3343
Website: www.tuitionedge.com
Eligibility: either the purchaser or the beneficiary must be resident but no age
    requirements
State tax: favorable at distribution
Minimum/Maximum: $15 min.; $297,000 max.

Fees: no application fee; no maintenance fee for state residents
Management: Delaware Investments
Other: investment options available

Idaho College Savings Program (IDeal)

Type: college savings
Phone: 866-433-2533
Website: www.idsaves.org
Eligibility: no residency or age requirements
State tax: deductible contributions within limits; favorable at distribution
Minimum/Maximum: $25 min.; $235,000 per beneficiary
Fees: no
Management: TIAA/CREF Tuition Financing, Inc.
Other: investment options available

College Illinois—529 Prepaid Tuition Program

Type: prepaid tuition
Phone: 877-877-3724
Website: www.collegeillinois.com
Eligibility: owner or beneficiary must be resident at least twelve months prior to
    purchase; no distribution for at least three years
State tax: favorable at distribution
Minimum/Maximum: $1,086 min.; $33,983 max.
Fees: $85 application fee
Management: Illinois Student Assistance Commission
Other: various payment options

Illinois Bright Start Savings

Type: college savings
Phone: 877-432-7444
Website: www.brightstartsavings.com
Eligibility: no residency or age requirements
State tax: deductible contributions; favorable at distribution
Minimum/Maximum: $25 min.; $235,000 max.
Fees: no, unless opened through a bank, then $30 application fee
Management: Citigroup Asset Management
Other: investment options available

Indiana College Choice Investment Plan

Type: college savings
Phone: 866-400-7526
Website: www.collegechoiceplan.com
Eligibility: no residency or age requirements
State tax: favorable at distribution
Minimum/Maximum: $50 min.; $236,750 max.
Fees: $10 application fee for out-of-state residents only; $10 in-state and $30 out-
    of-state annual maintenance fee

Management: One Group Investments
Other: investment options available

College Savings Iowa

Type: college savings
Phone: 800-672-9116
Website: www.collegesavingsiowa.com
Eligibility: no residency requirements; recipient must be under eighteen when
   account is established
State tax: qualified contributions deductible; favorable at distribution
Minimum/Maximum: $50 min.; $239,000 max.
Fees: no
Management: State Treasurer, Vanguard
Other: investment options available; Iowa announced in 2003 a separate, employer-
   based payroll college-savings plan called "The Principal"

Kansas Learning Quest Education Savings Program

Type: college savings
Phone: 800-579-2203
Website: www.learningquestsavings.com
Eligibility: no residency or age requirements
State tax: favorable
Minimum/Maximum: $2,500 min.; $235,000 max.
Fees: no application fee but annual maintenance fee of $27 under certain conditions
   for out-of-state residents
Management: American Century Investment Management, Inc.
Other: investment options available

Kentucky Education Savings Plan Trust

Type: college savings
Phone: 877-598-7878
Website: www.kysaves.com
Eligibility: no residency or age requirements
State tax: Qualified contributions deductible; favorable at distribution
Minimum/Maximum: $25 min.; $235,000 max.
Fees: no
Management: TIAA/CREF Tuition Financing, Inc.
Other: investment options available

Kentucky's Affordable Prepaid Tuition Plan (KAPT)

Type: prepaid tuition
Phone: 888-919-5278
Website: www.getkapt.com
Eligibility: beneficiary must be resident at time of purchase and intend to enroll in
   a Kentucky institution; purchase contract at least two years before distribution
State tax: favorable for qualified distributions

Minimum/Maximum: $1,930 min.; $68,885 max.
Fees: $50 application fee
Management: KAPT Board of Directors and Office of State Treasurer
Other: various packages available and payment-plan options

Louisiana State Tuition Assistance and Revenue Trust (START)
Type: college savings
Phone: 800-259-5626
Website: www.osfa.state.la.us
Eligibility: either account owner or beneficiary must be resident; no age requirement
State tax: qualified contributions; favorable at distribution
Minimum/Maximum: $10 min.; $197,600 max.
Fees: no
Management: Louisiana State Treasurer
Other: investment options available

Maine NextGen College Investment Plan
Type: college savings
Phone: 877-463-9843
Website: www.nextgenplan.com
Eligibility: no residency or age requirements
State tax: Some qualified contributions; favorable at distribution
Minimum/Maximum: $250 min.; $250,000 max.
Fees: no application fee; $50 annual fee for out-of-state residents under certain conditions
Management: Merrill Lynch
Other: investment options available

College Savings Plans of Maryland—Prepaid College Trust
Type: prepaid
Phone: 888-463-4723
Website: www.collegesavingsmd.org
Eligibility: owner or beneficiary must be resident of Maryland or D.C.; beneficiary must be in 9th grade or below at time of purchase
State tax: qualified deductions; favorable at distribution
Minimum/Maximum: $5,435 min.; $31,992 max.
Fees: $75 application fee
Management: Maryland Higher Education Investment Board
Other: various packages available and payment options available

College Savings Plans of Maryland—College Investment Plan
Type: college savings
Phone: 888-919-5278
Website: www.collegesavingsmd.org
Eligibility: no residency or age requirements
State tax: qualified contributions deductible; favorable at distribution

Minimum/Maximum: $250 min.; $250,000 max.
Fees: $90 application fee; $30 annual maintenance can be waived
Management: T. Rowe Price Associates
Other: Investment options available

Massachusetts University Fund College Investing Plan

Type: college savings
Phone: 800-544-2776
Website: http://personal.fidelity.com
Eligibility: no residency or age requirements
State tax: favorable at distribution
Minimum/Maximum: $1,000 min.; $230,000 max.
Fees: no application fee; $30 annual maintenance fee waived with automatic contributions
Management: Fidelity Investments
Other: investment options available

Massachusetts University Plan

Type: prepaid tuition
Phone: 800-449-6332
Website: www.mefa.org
Eligibility: no residency requirement; beneficiary must be related to owner; beneficiary must attend one of over eighty participating institutions in Massachusetts
State tax: favorable at distribution
Minimum/Maximum: $300 min.; max. is cost of tuition and fees times four of highest-cost participating school
Fees: no
Management: Massachusetts Educational Financing Authority
Other: various packages available; lump-sum only payment

Michigan Education Trust (MET)

Type: prepaid tuition
Phone: 800-638-4543
Website: www.michigan.gov/treasury
Eligibility: beneficiary must be state resident; grade level requirements based on MET program
State tax: contributions deductible; favorable at distribution
Minimum/Maximum: $1,730 min.; $24,252 max.
Fees: application fee ranges from $25 to $85
Management: MET Board of Directors and Department of Treasury
Other: various tuition packages available as well as payment options

Michigan Education Savings Program

Type: college savings
Phone: 877-861-6377
Website: www.misaves.com
Eligibility: no residency or age requirements
State tax: qualified favorable deductions; favorable at distribution

Minimum/Maximum: $25 min.; $235,000 max. per beneficiary
Fees: no
Management: TIAA/CREF Tuition Financing, Inc.
Other: investment options available

Minnesota College Savings Plan
Type: college savings
Phone: 877-338-4646
Website: www.mnsaves.org
Eligibility: no residency or age requirements
State tax: Provides up to $300 matching grant per year for qualifying families based on income
Minimum/Maximum: $25 min.; $235,000 max.
Fees: no
Management: TIAA/CREF Tuition Financing, Inc.
Other: investment options available

Mississippi Prepaid Affordable College Tuition (MPACT) Program
Type: prepaid tuition
Phone: 800-987-4450
Website: www.treasury.state.ms.us
Eligibility: beneficiary must be state resident and eighteen years or younger at time of purchase
State tax: qualified contributions; favorable at distribution
Minimum/Maximum: $1,229 min.; $19,580 max.
Fees: $60
Management: Mississippi Treasury Department
Other: various tuition packages available as well as payment options

Mississippi Affordable College Savings (MASC) Program
Type: college savings
Phone: 800-486-3670
Website: www.collegesavingsms.com
Eligibility: no state residency or age requirements
State tax: qualified deductions; favorable at distribution
Minimum/Maximum: $25 min.; $235,000 max.
Fees: no
Management: TIAA/CREF Tuition Financing, Inc.
Other: investment options available

Missouri Saving for Tuition (MO$T) Program
Type: college savings
Phone: 888-414-6678
Website: www.missourimost.org
Eligibility: no residency or age requirements
State tax: Qualified deductions; favorable at distribution
Minimum/Maximum: $25 min.; $235,000 max.

Fees: no
Management: TIAA/CREF Tuition Financing, Inc.
Other: investment options available

Montana Family Education Savings Program
Type: college savings
Phone: 800-888-2723
Website: http://montana.collegesavings.com
Eligibility: no residency or age requirements
State tax: qualified deductions; favorable at distribution
Minimum/Maximum: $250 min.; $262,000 max.
Fees: no
Management: College Savings Bank
Other: available investment options

Montana Pacific Funds 529 College Savings Plan
Type: college savings
Phone: 800-888-2723
Website: www.pacificlife.com
Eligibility: must be resident to purchase; no age requirement for beneficiary
State tax: Qualified contribution deductions; favorable at distribution
Minimum/Maximum: $500 min.; $249,000 max.
Fees: no
Management: College Savings Bank
Other: limited investment options available

College Savings Plan of Nebraska
Type: college savings
Phone: 888-993-3746
Website: www.planforcollegenow.com
Eligibility: no residency or age requirements
State tax: Qualified deductions; favorable at distribution
Minimum/Maximum: $0 min.; $250,000 max.
Fees: $5 per quarter maintenance fee; no application fee
Management: Union Bank & Trust Company
Other: investment options available

Nebraska Aim College Savings Plan
Type: college savings
Phone: 877-246-7526
Website: www.aiminvestments.com
Eligibility: no residency or age requirements
State tax: qualified contributions deductible; favorable at distribution
Minimum/Maximum: $25 min.; $250,000 max.
Fees: $25 annual maintenance fee can be waived
Management: Union Bank & Trust Company and AIM
Other: limited investment options available

Nebraska State Farm College Savings Plan

Type: college savings
Phone: 877-246-2526
Website: www.statefarm.com
Eligibility: no residency or age requirements
State tax: qualified contributions deductible; favorable at distribution
Minimum/Maximum: $500 min.; $250,000 max.
Fees: $25 annual maintenance fee can be waived
Management: Union Bank & Trust Company and AIM
Other: investment options available

Nebraska TD Waterhouse College Savings Plan

Type: college savings
Phone: 877-408-4644
Website: www.tdwaterhouse.com
Eligibility: no residency or age requirements
State tax: qualified contributions deductible; favorable at distribution
Minimum/Maximum: $0 min.; $250,000 max.
Fees: $7.50 quarterly maintenance fee
Management: Union Bank & Trust Company
Other: investment options available

Nevada Prepaid Tuition Program

Type: prepaid tuition
Phone: 888-477-2667
Website: www.nevadatreasurer.com
Eligibility: beneficiary or owner must be state resident at time of purchase or owner must be alumnus of Nevada College; age and grade limitations also
State tax: N/A; no Nevada income tax
Minimum/Maximum: $3,010 min.; $13,450 max.
Fees: $100 application fee
Management: Board of Trustees of the College Savings Plan of Nevada and the State Treasurer's Office
Other: various tuition packages available as well as payment options

American Skandia College Savings Plan (Nevada)

Type: college savings
Phone: 800-752-6342
Website: www2.americanskandia.com
Eligibility: no
State tax: N/A; no Nevada income tax
Minimum/Maximum: $250 min.; $250,000 max.
Fees: $30 annual maintenance fee can be waived
Management: Strong Capital Management, Inc.
Other: investment options available

Nevada Strong 529 Plan
Type: college savings
Phone: 877-529-5295
Website: www.estrong.com
Eligibility: no residency or age requirements
State tax: N/A; no Nevada income tax
Minimum/Maximum: $250 min.; $250,000 max.
Fees: $10 application fee; $10 maintenance fee
Management: Strong Capital Management, Inc.
Other: investment options available

Nevada Upromise College Fund
Type: college savings
Phone: 800-587-7305
Website: www.upromise.com
Eligibility: no residency or age requirements
State tax: N/A; no Nevada income tax
Minimum/Maximum: $250 min.; $250,000 max.
Fees: $20 annual maintenance fee
Management: Upromise Investments, Inc.
Other: investment options available

Nevada USAA College Savings Plan
Type: college savings
Phone: 800-645-6268
Website: www.lc.usaa.com
Eligibility: no residency or age requirements
State tax: N/A; no Nevada income tax
Minimum/Maximum: $2,000 min.; $250,000 max.
Fees: $30 annual maintenance fee
Management: Strong Capital Management, Inc.
Other: investment options available

Nevada Vanguard 529 Savings Plan
Type: college savings
Phone: 866-734-4530
Website: www.vanguard.com
Eligibility: no residency or age requirements
State tax: N/A; no Nevada income tax
Minimum/Maximum: $3,000 min.; $250,000 max.
Fees: no
Management: Upromise Investments, Inc.
Other: investment options available

Nevada Columbia 529 Plan
Type: college savings
Phone: 877-994-2529
Website: www.columbiafunds.com
Eligibility: no residency or age requirements
State tax: N/A; no Nevada income tax
Minimum/Maximum: $1,000 min.; $250,000 max.
Fees: $25 annual maintenance fee
Management: Columbia Management Group
Other: investment options available

New Hampshire Fidelity Advisor 529 Plan
Type: college savings
Phone: 800-522-7297
Website: https://advisorxpress.fidelity.com
Eligibility: no residency or age requirements
State tax: favorable at distribution
Minimum/Maximum: $1,000 min.; $250,000 max.
Fees: $30 annual maintenance fee under certain conditions
Management: Fidelity Investments
Other: investment options available

New Hampshire UNIQUE College Investing Plan
Type: college savings
Phone: 800-544-1722
Website: http://personal.fidelity.com
Eligibility: no residency or age requirements
State tax: favorable for qualified distributions
Minimum/Maximum: $1,000 min.; $250,000 max.
Fees: $30 annual maintenance fee can be waived
Management: Fidelity Investments
Other: investment options available

New Jersey 529 College Savings Plan (NJBEST)
Type: college savings
Phone: 877-465-2378
Website: www.njbest.com
Eligibility: purchaser or beneficiary must be resident at time of initial purchase
State tax: favorable upon distribution; up to $1,500 scholarship available to New
    Jersey beneficiaries at New Jersey institution
Minimum/Maximum: $300 min.; $305,000 max.
Fees: no
Management: Franklin Templeton Distributors, Inc.
Other: investment options available

New Jersey Franklin Templeton 529 College Savings Plan

Type: Savings
Phone: 800-223-2141
Website: www.franklintempleton.com
Eligibility: no residency or age requirements
State tax: certain New Jersey beneficiaries could receive up to $1,500 scholarship; favorable at qualified distributions
Minimum/Maximum: $250 min.; $305,000 max.
Fees: $25 annual maintenance fee can be waived
Management: Franklin Templeton Distributors, Inc.
Other: investment options available

The New Mexico Education Plan's Prepaid Tuition Program

Type: prepaid tuition
Phone: 877-337-5268
Website: www.tepnm.com
Eligibility: account owner or beneficiary must be state resident; contract must be purchased at least five years prior to disbursement
State tax: favorable for deduction and at distribution
Minimum/Maximum: min.: one year of undergraduate tuition in New Mexico; max.: five year of undergraduate tuition in New Mexico
Fees: no
Management: Schoolhouse Capital, a division of State Street Corporation
Other: various tuition packages available; payment options

The New Mexico Education Plan's College Savings Program

Type: college savings
Phone: 877-337-5268
Website: www.theeducationplan.com
Eligibility: no residency or age requirement
State tax: favorable for deduction and at distribution
Minimum/Maximum: $250 min.; $294,000 max.
Fees: no application fee but annual $30 maintenance fee under certain conditions
Management: Schoolhouse Capital, a division of State Street Corporation
Other: investment options available

New Mexico Scholar's Edge

Type: college savings
Phone: 866-529-7283
Website: www.scholarsedge529.com
Eligibility: no residency or age requirements
State tax: contributions deductible; favorable at distribution
Minimum/Maximum: $250 min.; $294,000 max.
Fees: $25 annual maintenance fee can be waived
Management: Schoolhouse Capital
Other: investment options available

New Mexico CollegeSense 529 Higher Education Savings Plan
Type: college savings
Phone: 866-529-7367
Website: www.collegesense.com
Eligibility: no residency or age requirements
State tax: deductible contributions; favorable at distribution
Minimum/Maximum: $500 min.; $294,000 max.
Fees: $25 annual maintenance fee can be waived
Management: Schoolhouse Capital
Other: investment options available

New Mexico Arrive Education Savings Plan
Type: college savings
Phone: 877-277-4838
Website: www.arrive529.com
Eligibility: no residency or age requirements
State tax: contributions deductible; favorable at distribution
Minimum/Maximum: $250 min.; $294,000 max.
Fees: $25 annual maintenance fee can be waived
Management: Schoolhouse Capital
Other: investment options available

New York College Savings Program
Type: college savings
Phone: 877-697-2837
Website: http://nysaves.uii.upromise.com
Eligibility: no residency or age requirements
State tax: qualified deductions; favorable at distribution
Minimum/Maximum: $25 min.; $235,000 max.
Fees: no
Management: The Vanguard Group
Other: investment options available

North Carolina National College Savings Program
Type: college savings
Phone: 800-600-3453
Website: www.cfnc.org/savings
Eligibility: state residency or other limited relationship with state
State tax: favorable for qualified distribution
Minimum/Maximum: $5 min.; $276,046 max.
Fees: no
Management: College Foundation, Inc.
Other: investment options available

North Dakota College Save
Type: college savings
Phone: 866-728-3529
Website: www.collegesave4u.com
Eligibility: no residency or age requirements
State tax: favorable at distribution
Minimum/Maximum: $25 min.; $269,000 max.
Fees: no
Management: Morgan Stanley
Other: investment options available

Ohio College Advantage Savings Plan
Type: college savings
Phone: 800-233-6734
Website: www.collegeadvantage.com
Eligibility: either account owner or beneficiary must be state resident
State tax: qualified deductions; favorable for qualified distribution
Minimum/Maximum: $15 min.; $245,000 max.
Fees: no
Management: Putnam Investments
Other: investment options available

Ohio Putnam CollegeAdvantage Savings Plan
Type: college savings
Phone: 800-225-1581
Website: www.putnaminvestments.com
Eligibility: no residency or age requirements
State tax: qualified contribution deductions; favorable qualified distributions
Minimum/Maximum: $25 min.; $245,000 max.
Fees: $25 annual maintenance fee can be waived
Management: Putnam Investments
Other: investment options available

Ohio CollegeAdvantage—Guaranteed Option
Type: Guaranteed Savings
Phone: 800-233-6734
Website: www.collegeadvantage.com
Eligibility: owner or beneficiary must be state resident
State tax: qualified contribution deductible; favorable qualified distributions
Minimum/Maximum: $15 min.; $245,000 max.
Fees: no
Management: Ohio Tuition Trust Authority
Other: $95 cost per unit

Oklahoma College Savings Plan

Type: college savings
Phone: 877-654-7284
Website: www.ok4saving.org
Eligibility: no residency or age requirements
State tax: qualified deductions; favorable at distribution
Minimum/Maximum: $25 min.; $235,000 max.
Fees: no
Management: TIAA/CREF Tuition Financing, Inc.
Other: investment options available

Oregon College Savings Plan

Type: college savings
Phone: 866-772-8464
Website: www.estrong.com
Eligibility: no residency or age requirements
State tax: qualified deductions; favorable at distribution
Minimum/Maximum: $250 min.; $250,000 max.
Fees: no application fee; annual $30 maintenance fee under certain conditions
Management: TBA
Other: investment options available

Oregon MFS Savings Plan

Type: college savings
Phone: 866-637-7526
Website: www.mfs.com
Eligibility: no residency or age requirements
State tax: qualified contributions under certain limits; favorable at distribution
Minimum/Maximum: $250 min.; $250,000 max.
Fees: no application fee; $25 annual maintenance fee waived for residents
Management: MFS Investment Management
Other: investment options available

Oregon USA College Connect

Type: college savings
Phone: 800-457-9001
Website: www.usacollegeconnect.com
Eligibility: no residency or age requirements
State tax: qualified contributions deductible; favorable for qualified distributions
Minimum/Maximum: min. varies; max. N/A
Fees: $30 annual maintenance fee can be waived
Management: Schoolhouse Capital
Other: investment options available

Pennsylvania TAP 529 Guaranteed Savings Plan

Type: prepaid unit/guaranteed savings
Phone: 880-440-4000
Website: www.lfg.com
Eligibility: account owner or beneficiary must be state resident; no age requirement
State tax: consult TAP 529 for special provisions
Minimum/Maximum: $25 min.; $290,000 max.
Fees: $50 application fee; $25 annual fee; both fees adjustable
Management: Pennsylvania State Treasury
Other: investment options available

Pennsylvania TAP 529 Investment Plan

Type: college savings
Phone: 800-440-4000
Website: www.lfg.com
Eligibility: account owner or beneficiary must be state resident; no age requirement
State tax: favorable for qualified distributions
Minimum/Maximum: $1,000 min.; $290,000 max.
Fees: no application fee; $25 annual maintenance fee can be waived under certain conditions
Management: Delaware Investments
Other: investment options available

Rhode Island College Bound Fund

Type: college savings
Phone: 888-324-5057
Website: www.collegeboundfund.com
Eligibility: residency requirements but no age requirements
State tax: qualified deductions and up to $500 matching funds from program under certain conditions for some families; favorable at distribution
Minimum/Maximum: $250 min.; $301,550 max.
Fees: no
Management: Alliance Capital
Other: investment options available

Rhode Island JP Morgan Higher Education Plan

Type: college savings
Phone: 877-576-3529
Website: http://jpmorganfleming.chase.com
Eligibility: no residency or age requirements
State tax: qualified contributions deductible; favorable at distribution
Minimum/Maximum: $1,000 min.; $301,550 max.
Fees: $25 annual maintenance fee can be waived
Management: Alliance Capital, JP Morgan Investment Management
Other: investment options available

South Carolina Tuition Payment Plan
Type: prepaid tuition
Phone: 888-772-4723
Website: www.scgrad.org
Eligibility: beneficiary must be state resident at least twelve months before disbursement and be in 10th grade or below at time of purchase
State tax: contributions deductible and favorable for qualified distributions
Minimum/Maximum: $10,061 min.; $21,828 max.
Fees: $75 application fee
Management: State Treasurer
Other: tuition packages and payment options available

South Carolina Future Scholar 529 Savings Plan
Type: college savings
Phone: 888-244-5674
Website: www.futurescholar.com
Eligibility: owner or beneficiary must be state residents at time of purchase; also available to certain others; no age requirement
State tax: contributions deductible and favorable for qualified distributions
Minimum/Maximum: $250 min.; $265,000 max.
Fees: no
Management: Bank of America Advisors, LLC
Other: investment options available

South Dakota CollegeAccess 529
Type: college savings
Phone: 866-529-7462
Website: www.collegeaccess529.com
Eligibility: owner or beneficiary must be state resident; no age requirement
State tax: N/A, no South Dakota income tax
Minimum/Maximum: $250 min.; $305,000 max.
Fees: no
Management: PIMCO Funds Distributors, LLC
Other: investment options available

South Dakota Legg Mason Core4College 529 Plan
Type: college savings
Phone: 800-800-3609
Website: www.leggmason.com
Eligibility: no residency or age requirements
State tax: no South Dakota income tax
Minimum/Maximum: $1,000 min.; $305,000 max.
Fees: $25 annual maintenance fee can be waived
Management: PIMCO Advisors Distributors, LLC
Other: investment options available

Tennessee BEST Prepaid Tuition Plan

Type: prepaid tuition
Phone: 888-486-2378
Website: www.treasury.state.tn.us/best
Eligibility: owner or beneficiary must be state resident; no age requirement
State tax: contributions deductible; N/A, no Tennessee personal income tax
Minimum/Maximum: $42 min.; $235,000 max.
Fees: no
Management: Treasury Department and Board Chaired by State Treasurer
Other: various payment options

Tennessee BEST Saving Plan

Type: college savings
Phone: 888-486-2378
Website: www.tnbest.com
Eligibility: no
State tax: contributions deductible; no Tennessee personal income tax
Minimum/Maximum: $25 min.; $235,000 max.
Fees: no
Management: TIAA/CREF Tuition Financing, Inc.
Other: investment options available

Texas Tomorrow's Investment Plan

Type: college savings
Phone: 800-445-4723
Website: www.enterprise529.com
Eligibility: owner or beneficiary must be state resident; no age requirement
State tax: N/A; no state income tax
Minimum/Maximum: $25 min.; $257,460 max.
Fees: no
Management: Enterprise Capital Management, Inc.
Other: investment options available

Utah Educational Savings Plan (UESP) Trust

Type: college savings
Phone: 800-418-2551
Website: www.uesp.org
Eligibility: no
State tax: qualified deductions under certain conditions; favorable at distribution
Minimum/Maximum: $25 min.; $260,000 max.
Fees: no application fee but annual maintenance variable rate fee based on fund
 value
Management: State Agency
Other: investment options available

Vermont Higher Education Investment Plan

Type: college savings
Phone: 800-637-5860
Website: www.vsac.org
Eligibility: no
State tax: favorable at distribution; state residents may be eligible for limited additional consideration
Minimum/Maximum: $25 min.; $240,100 max.
Fees: no
Management: TIAA/CREF Tuition Financing, Inc.
Other: investment options available

Virginia College America

Type: college savings
Phone: 800-421-4120
Website: www.americanfunds.com
Eligibility: no
State tax: limited contributions deductible under certain conditions; favorable at distribution
Minimum/Maximum: $250 min.; $250,000 max.
Fees: $10 application fee and $10 annual maintenance fee
Management: Virginia College Savings Plan; American Funds
Other: limited investment options available

Virginia Prepaid Education Program (VPEP)

Type: prepaid tuition
Phone: 888-567-0540
Website: www.virginia529.com
Eligibility: account owner, beneficiary, or parent of beneficiary must be state resident; beneficiary must be in 9th grade or lower at purchase
State tax: limited contributions deductible under certain conditions; favorable at distribution
Minimum/Maximum: $1,505 min.; $34,593 max.
Fees: $85 application fee
Management: Virginia College Savings Plan Board and its Executive Director
Other: tuition packages and payment options available

Virginia Education Savings Trust (VEST)

Type: college savings
Phone: 888-567-0540
Website: www.virginia529.com
Eligibility: no
State tax: limited contributions deductible under certain conditions; favorable at distribution
Minimum/Maximum: $250 min.; $250,000 max.
Fees: $85 application fee

Management: Virginia College Savings Plan Board and its Executive Director
Other: investment options available

Washington Guaranteed Education Tuition (GET)

Type: prepaid unit; guaranteed savings
Phone: 877-438-8848
Website: www.get.wa.gov
Eligibility: beneficiary must be state resident; no age requirement
State tax: N/A; no Washington income tax
Minimum/Maximum: min. $57 per unit; max. $28,500 for 500 units
Fees: $50 application fee
Management: Washington State Higher Education Coordinating Board
Other: 100 units guarantee of in-state tuition and fees at highest-priced public
university in Washington

West Virginia SMART529 College Savings Option

Type: college savings
Phone: 866-574-3542
Website: www.hartfordinvestor.com
Eligibility: no residency or age requirements
State tax: contributions deductible; favorable at distribution
Minimum/Maximum: $100 min.; $265,620 max.
Fees: no
Management: Hartford Life Insurance Company, Inc.
Other: investment options available

West Virginia SMART529 College Savings Option

Type: college savings
Phone: 866-574-3542
Website: www.hartfordinvestor.com
Eligibility: owner or beneficiary must be state resident; no age requirement
State tax: contributions deductible; favorable at distribution
Minimum/Maximum: $100 min.; $265,620 max.
Fees: no
Management: Hartford Life Insurance Company, Inc.
Other: investment options available

West Virginia Leaders SMART529

Type: college savings
Phone: 866-574-3542
Website: www.hartfordinvestor.com
Eligibility: no residency or age requirements
State tax: contributions deductible; favorable at distribution
Minimum/Maximum: $500 min.; $265,620 max.
Fees: $25 annual maintenance fee can be waived
Management: Hartford Life Insurance Company, Inc.
Other: investment options available

Wisconsin EdVest

Type: college savings
Phone: 888-338-3789
Website: www.estrong.com
Eligibility: no residency or age requirements
State tax: qualified contributions deductible; favorable at distribution
Minimum/Maximum: $250 min.; $246,000 max.
Fees: $10 application fee; $10 annual maintenance fee; both fees can be waived under certain conditions
Management: Strong Management Capital, Inc.
Other: investment options available

Wyoming College Achievement Program

Type: college savings
Phone: 877-529-2655
Website: www.collegeachievementplan.com
Eligibility: no residency or age requirements
State tax: N/A; no Wyoming income tax
Minimum/Maximum: $250 min.; $245,000 max.
Fees: no application fees; $25 annual maintenance fee can be waived under certain conditions
Management: Mercury Advisors
Other: investment options available

Independent 529 Plan (The Tuition Plan Consortium)

Type: prepaid tuition
Phone: 888-718-7878
Website: www.independent529plan.com
Eligibility: no residency requirements; minimum three years before disbursement
State tax: no favorable state tax consideration
Minimum/Maximum: $500 min.; max. five times the annual tuition and fees of the highest-cost participating institution
Fees: no
Management: TIAA/CREF Tuition Financing, Inc.
Other: each participating institution offers at least half of 1 percent discount from current costs in lieu of the state 529 programs' favorable state-tax consideration

GET UPDATED!

A number of 529 Prepaid Tuition Plans offered by states have been suspended in recent months. These include Colorado, Kentucky, Ohio, Texas, and West Virginia. Individuals who are interested in these programs should inquire directly with each state's program to learn about current plans for the future of each particular program. In addition, each state is regularly reviewing the individual provisions for its 529 program(s). These include eligibility criteria, tax considerations, program management, fees, and contribution levels. Typically, the best source for up-to-date information can be secured from the program's website or its toll-free number.

One final thought as you proceed: Although most of these 529 programs are not directly regulated by the Securities and Exchange Commission (SEC) because they are managed by state governments, many states have contracted with fund managers who invest funds on behalf of the state trust and, ultimately, the participant. While many 529 plans invest in mutual funds, the SEC has found that most 529 investors receive less information regarding their investments than if they had directly purchased shares of a mutual fund on their own. The SEC has thus established a special task force to review cost and management issues, including the transparency of financial and investment information, disclosure of information to investors, and accountability for fund management.

As is suggested by the varying range of fees provided in the summaries below, participants should investigate and compare both sign-up fees and annual maintenance costs.

APPENDIX B: 529 CHECKLIST

ELIGIBILITY

- Can anyone open an account?
- Who qualifies as a beneficiary?
- Can the purchaser or beneficiary be an out-of-state resident?
- What happens if the purchaser or beneficiary moves out of state?
- Can a beneficiary have more than one 529 plan?
- Is there a minimum or maximum age for the beneficiary?

PURCHASE

- Can the plan be purchased directly from the state or through a second party, such as an investment broker?
- If purchased through a broker, is there a special fee for application and/or for annual maintenance?
- If there is a broker option for purchase, is there a choice of brokers and, if not, why?
- What is the level of service provided by the plan—i.e., reports, electronic communication, toll-free numbers?
- Can anyone else other than the initial purchaser contribute to a 529 plan?
- Can a purchaser own more than one 529 plan?

LIMITATIONS

- At what institution(s) can the 529 plan be used?
- Are the institutions being considered for the beneficiary eligible to participate in the 529 plan?
- Is there a minimum amount required to participate?
- Is there a maximum amount that can be contributed?

- Is there a time frame for participation in the 529 program before any distribution can be made?
- Are there any restrictions for use of the funds (that is, tuition and fees, room and board, undergraduate, full-time status)?

FEES

- What fees are charged, if any, for application and for annual maintenance of the account?
- What are the fees taken from the investment return by the 529 program?
- What are the penalties for withdrawals taken from the account if the funds are not used for qualified expenses?
- Is there a fee assessed for changing beneficiaries?
- Is there a fee if the account is closed?

TAXES

- Does the program comply with federal income tax exemptions?
- Does the 529 program provide any additional considerations such as deduction of contributions from state taxable income or with favorable state income-tax exemption at distribution?

OTHER BENEFITS

- Are there any other special benefits associated with the 529 plan such as matching contributions for certain families from the provider?
- Is there a scholarship competition available for participants?
- Does the 529 program provide any other special considerations such as a tuition discount; if so, for how much?

INVESTMENT

- Will there be a guarantee and, if so, who is the guarantor and what are the conditions?
- Is there an investment choice, and, if so, what are the conditions?
- Are there various payment options?
- Is there any risk?
- What is the program's investment record to date?
- Has the program been stable since inception or have there been interruptions?
- What happens if the program's investment manager changes?

APPENDIX C

Identifying the Resources for Meeting College Costs

	Average Four Year Public Institution	Average Four Year Private Institution	Your School
Cost of Attendance	$15,000	$28,000	
Resources			Your Resources
Parent Contribution from Savings	$4,000	$4,000	
Parent Contribution from Current Income	$3,000	$3,000	
Student Contribution from Savings	$1,000	$1,000	
Student Contribution from Summer Job	$1,500	$1,500	
Student Contribution from Campus Job	$2,000	$2,000	
Local and State Scholarships	$1,000	$1,000	
Unsubsidized Stafford Loan or PLUS Loan	$2,500	$2,500	
Total Resources			Your Total Resources
			Subtract Cost from Resources
Cost Less Resources	$15,000	$15,000	
Remaining Need	── 0 ──	$13,000	Your Remaining Need

Need-based aid or receipt of an institutional merit scholarship could meet remaining need.

When considering payment scenarios, remember that flexibility is important. As costs increase, consider additional options. Some or all of the parent and/or student contribution could be secured by paying over time via one of several alternatives.

APPENDIX D

College Cost Savings Estimate Tools

College Cost Inflation

Predicting college cost inflation from one year to the next is a challenge. Trying to predict it for several years into the future is an even greater challenge. Without a crystal ball, the best estimates made today will surely need to be refined annually. The following Inflation Factor charts will help you estimate, with Inflation Factors ranging from 5 percent to 9 percent annual rate increases.

Inflation Factors

Years to Start College	Inflation Rate				
	5 percent	6 percent	7 percent	8 percent	9 percent
1	1.10	1.12	1.07	1.08	1.09
2	1.16	1.19	1.15	1.17	1.19
3	1.22	1.26	1.23	1.59	1.30
4	1.28	1.34	1.31	1.71	1.41
5	1.34	1.42	1.40	1.85	1.54
6	1.41	1.50	1.50	2.00	1.68
7	1.48	1.59	1.61	2.16	1.83
8	1.55	1.69	1.72	2.33	1.99
9	1.63	1.70	1.84	2.52	2.17
10	1.71	1.90	1.97	2.72	2.40
11	1.80	2.01	2.11	2.94	2.58
12	1.89	2.13	2.25	3.17	2.81
13	1.98	2.26	2.41	3.42	3.07
14	2.08	2.40	2.58	3.70	3.34
15	2.19	2.54	2.76	3.99	3.64
16	2.29	2.69	2.95	4.31	3.97
17	2.41	2.84	3.16	4.66	4.33
18	2.53	3.03	3.62	5.03	4.72

Return on Investment

By investing on a regular basis, you'll become better at spending your resources, setting your financial priorities, and instilling a sense of discipline. Regardless of what is initially established, wise investors will regularly reassess their abilities to stay on track for the long-term periods envisioned. There surely are numerous factors, some positive, that could or should result in adjustments for either greater or smaller payments.

You can't use a crystal ball in terms of predicting the future world of investments. However, the longer the time span involved, the less impact unusual peaks and valleys in the marketplace will have on your long-term goal.

The Historical Annualized Returns chart for the last fifty years may help you decide on what reasonable set of assumptions you may want to consider. The Return Rate Factor chart allows you to select annualized rates of return ranging from 6 percent to 10 percent.

Historical Annualized Returns for Fifty Years

Decade	S&P 500 Index Annual Returns
1950 to 1959	13.4 percent
1960 to 1969	5.2 percent
1970 to 1979	2.4 percent
1980 to 1989	12.0 percent
1990 to 1999	16.1 percent
	9.8 percent (Average ten-year return)

Source: Media General Financial Services (S&P 500 data)

Return Rate Factors
Interest Compounded Annually

Years to Start College	Return Rate				
	6 percent	7 percent	8 percent	9 percent	10 percent
1	0.60	0.70	0.80	0.90	1.00
2	1.24	1.45	1.66	1.88	2.10
3	1.91	2.25	2.60	2.95	3.31
4	2.63	3.11	3.61	4.12	4.64
5	3.38	4.03	4.69	5.39	6.10
6	4.19	5.01	5.87	6.77	7.71
7	5.04	6.06	7.14	8.28	9.49
8	5.94	7.18	8.51	9.93	11.43
9	6.90	8.39	9.99	11.72	13.58
10	7.91	9.67	11.59	13.67	15.94
11	8.98	11.05	13.32	15.80	18.53
12	10.12	12.52	15.18	18.13	21.38
13	11.33	14.10	17.20	20.66	24.52
14	12.61	15.79	19.37	23.42	27.98
15	13.97	17.59	21.72	26.43	31.77
16	15.40	19.52	24.26	29.70	35.95
17	16.93	21.59	27.00	33.28	40.55
18	18.54	23.80	29.96	37.17	45.60

WORKSHEET

The calculation worksheet on the next page will allow you to set up a savings program, the ultimate goal of which is intended to meet an estimate of resources need to help meet the college expenses of one student. It will require that you have the current costs of a particular institution. You will also need to select the appropriate information from the Inflation Factor chart and from the Return Rate Factor chart. An example is provided as an illustration to help better understand the process. By following these steps, you should be able to create a monthly savings plan.

Calculate the Cost

	Example	Your Child
1. Your child's age		
2. Years until the start of college (18 minus your child's age)	6	
3. Current annual cost of one year's tuition, fees, room & board a) enter your school's cost b) $10,636 (four-year public average) c) $26,854 (four-year private average)	12 $10,636	
4. College cost inflation factor (e.g., 7 percent) (choose one from the Inflation Factor chart)	2.25	
5. Future annual cost of college (step 3 times 4)	$23,931	
6. Future total cost of college (step 5 times years of college)	$95,724	

Assuming no savings at all upon starting the plan, how much should be saved on a monthly basis?

	Example	Your Child
7. Select a rate of annual return from the Return Rate chart (e.g., 10 percent)	21.38	
8. Calculate targeted annual amount to save by dividing step 6 by step 7	$4.477	
9. Monthly amount needed to be saved (divide step 8 by 12 months)	$373	

APPENDIX E

How Much Should Be Borrowed?

Trying to estimate what would be a reasonable amount of student loan indebtedness is not a perfectly scientific exercise. The following are a few of the many unknowns about the future that would be very difficult to know in advance:

- the on-time and successful completion of college by the student

- the cost of money and interest rates in the future

- the starting salary after college

- the level of responsibility for the loan obligation by the borrower

- other financial obligations

- plans for and the cost of further study after college

- possible loan repayment/forgiveness programs offered by the government or certain employers

- the changing demands for skills in the marketplace

- the promotional opportunities and salary adjustments of the borrower

- the debt load or wealth or income of future marriage partners

- the birth of children; their cost of education

- unusual and unexpected changes in health and employment

However, there are some general benchmarks that can provide some rough guidance.

- College graduates will earn nearly $1 million more over the course of their careers than people who have only a high school diploma.

- Students should not borrow more than is absolutely needed.

- Borrowing for college may be one of the best investments one could make in respect to impacting future economic well-being, health, and opportunities for enhancing prospects for a fuller life experience.

- While bankers may not all agree on what the right percent is for measuring a reasonable and manageable debt-to-income ratio, most would suggest that this rate would be between 8 percent to 12 percent.

So using a 10 percent debt-to-income ratio, the chart below provides some rough guidance on total student-loan balances and the income that would typically be needed to properly manage that debt reasonably.

Loan Balance	Monthly Payment*	Annual Salary Needed
$10,000	$123	$14,800
20,000	245	29,400
30,000	368	44,160
40,000	490	58,800
50,000	613	73,590

*Based upon an 8.25 percent interest rate and a ten-year repayment plan.

APPENDIX F

FM AND IM CALCULATIONS AND TABLES

Financial aid eligibility that is based upon the financial need of a student is determined by measuring a student's family's ability to pay for a given year of college. This "family ability to pay" figure is called the EFC, or Effective Family Contribution.

The EFC is subtracted from an institution's Cost of Attendance (COA) for a given year. The difference between the COA and the EFC is the individual student's financial need for a given year for a college.

There are two formulas or methodologies that are used to determine a student's EFC: the Federal Methodology (FM) and the Institutional Methodology (IM).

The FM is used by the federal and most state governments, as well as colleges, to determine eligibility for government student aid programs. The FM formula considers income, assets, expenses, family size, and other factors in its calculation of the EFC. The data for this calculation is obtained from the Free Application for Federal Student Aid (FAFSA), which must be submitted annually.

The IM calculation gathers all of the data submitted on the FAFSA as well as additional information about the family, including the equity in its home, an element not collected for the FM.

While the federal government is the largest single provider of student financial assistance, significant aid is also awarded by individual institutions and private organizations. The IM formula is employed by many colleges and organizations to determine student's eligibility for their own private funds, including scholarships. The IM data is collected through a separate, fee-based process by students and their families' annual completion of the CSS Financial Aid/PROFILE.

Both the FAFSA and the CSS Financial Aid/PROFILE may be found online and submitted to the appropriate agencies electronically (www.fafsa.ed.gov and www.collegeboard.com).

 **CollegeBoard**

ALLOWANCES FOR STATE AND OTHER TAXES			
	Parents of Dependent Students and Independent Students with Dependents other than a spouse		Dependent and Independent with No Dependents
	Total Income		**Total Income**
State/Territory/Country of Residence	$0-15,000	15,001-or more	Any amount
Alabama (AL)	3%	2%	2%
Alaska (AK)	2	1	0
American Samoa (AS)	3	2	2
Arizona (AZ)	4	3	3
Arkansas (AR)	3	2	3
California (CA)	6	5	5
Canada (CN)	3	2	2
Colorado (CO)	4	3	3
Connecticut (CT)	6	5	4
Delaware (DE)	4	3	3
District of Columbia (DC)	7	6	6
Federated States of Micronesia (FM)	3	2	2
Florida (FL)	2	1	0
Georgia (GA)	5	4	3
Guam (GU)	3	2	2
Hawaii (HI)	4	3	4
Idaho (ID)	5	4	4
Illinois (IL)	4	3	2
Indiana (IN)	4	3	3
Iowa (IA)	4	3	3
Kansas (KS)	4	3	3
Kentucky (KY)	5	4	4
Louisiana (LA)	2	1	1
Maine (ME)	6	5	4
Marshall Islands (MH)	3	2	2

2004-2005 FEDERAL METHODOLOGY (FM) COMPUTATION TABLES

continued

	Parents of Dependent Students and Independent Students with Dependents other than a spouse		Dependent and Independent with No Dependents
	Total Income		**Total Income**
Maryland (MD)	7	6	5
Massachusetts (MA)	6	5	4
Mexico (MX)	3	2	2
Michigan (MI)	5	4	3
Minnesota (MN)	6	5	4
Mississippi	3	2	2
Missouri (MO)	4	3	3
Montana (MT)	5	4	3
Nebraska (NE)	4%	3%	3%
Nevada (NV)	2	1	1
New Hampshire (NH)	4	3	1
New Jersey (NJ)	7	6	4
New Mexico (NM)	3	2	3
New York (NY)	8	7	5
North Carolina (NC)	5	4	4
North Dakota (ND)	2	1	1
Northern Mariana Islands (NP)	3	2	2
Ohio (OH)	5	4	4
Oklahoma (OK)	4	3	3
Oregon (OR)	7	6	5
Palau (PW)	3	2	2
Pennsylvania (PA)	4	3	3
Puerto Rico (PR)	3	2	2
Rhode Island (RI)	6	5	4
South Carolina (SC)	4	3	3
South Dakota (SD)	1	0	0
Tennessee (TN)	1	0	0
Texas (TX)	2	1	0
Utah (UT)	5	4	4

2004-2005 FEDERAL METHODOLOGY (FM)
COMPUTATION TABLES

	Parents of Dependent Students and Independent Students with Dependents other than a spouse		Dependent and Independent with No Dependents
	Total Income		Total Income
Vermont (VT)	5	4	3
Virgin Islands (VI)	3	2	2
Virginia (VA)	5	4	3
Washington (WA)	2	1	0
West Virginia (WV)	3	2	2
Wisconsin (WI)	6	5	4
Wyoming (WY)	1	0	0
Not Reported (NR)	3	2	2

ALLOWANCES AGAINST INCOME	
FICA: Wages	
$1 to $87,000	7.65% of income earned by each wage earner (maximum $6,655.50 per person)
$87,001 or more	$6,655.50 + 1.45% of income earned above $87,000 by each wage earner
Employment allowance	
35% of lesser earned income to a maximum of $3,000 (single parent: 35% of earned income to a maximum of $3,000)	

INCOME PROTECTION ALLOWANCE (IPA)
(Parents of Dependent Students/Independent Students with Dependents other than a spouse)

Family Size* (including student)	Number in College**				
	1	2	3	4	5
2	$13,700	$11,350			
3	$17,060	$14,730	$12,380		
4	$21,070	$18,720	$16,390	$14,050	
5	$24,860	$22,510	$20,180	$17,840	$15,510
6	$29,070	$26,730	$24,400	$22,060	$19,730

* For each additional family member, add $3,280.
** For each additional college student, subtract $2,330.

2004-2005 FEDERAL METHODOLOGY (FM) COMPUTATION TABLES

INCOME PROTECTION ALLOWANCE
(Dependent Students and Independent Students without Dependents)

Dependent Student	$2,420
Independent Student	4,490
Married Independent	(student and spouse enrolled)
5,490	Married Independent
(only student is enrolled)	8,780

ADJUSTED NET WORTH OF A BUSINESS OR FARM

Net Worth (NW)	Adjusted Net Worth
Less than $1	$0
$1 to 100,000	$0 + 40% of NW
$100,001 to 295,000	$40,000 + 50% of NW over $100,000
$295,001 to $490,000	$137,500 + 60% of NW over $295,000
$490,001 or more	$254,500 + 100% of NW over $490,000

2004-2005 FEDERAL METHODOLOGY (FM) COMPUTATION TABLES

ASSET PROTECTION ALLOWANCE *(Parents and Independent Students)*		
Age of older parent or student	Couple/Married	Unmarried/Single
25 or under	$0	$0
26	2,500	1,200
27	5,000	2,300
28	7,400	3,500
29	9,900	4,700
30	12,400	5,900
31	14,900	7,000
32	17,400	8,200
33	19,800	9,400
34	22,300	10,600
35	24,800	11,700
36	27,300	12,900
37	29,800	14,100
38	32,200	15,300
39	34,700	16,400
40	37,200	17,600
41	38,100	18,100
42	39,100	18,400
43	40,100	18,900
44	41,100	19,200
45	42,100	19,700
46	43,200	20,100
47	44,200	20,500
48	45,300	21,000
49	46,500	21,500
50	47,900	22,000
51	49,100	22,600
52	50,300	23,100
53	51,800	23,700

2004-2005 FEDERAL METHODOLOGY (FM) COMPUTATION TABLES

ASSET PROTECTION ALLOWANCE *(Parents and Independent Students)*		
Age of older parent or student	**Couple/Married**	**Unmarried/Single**
54	53,100	24,200
55	54,700	24,800
56	56,000	25,400
57	57,700	26,100
58	59,400	26,700
59	61,200	27,500
60	63,000	28,100
61	65,200	28,900
62	67,100	29,800
63	69,000	30,600
64	71,300	31,400
65 or over	73,700	32,300

ASSET CONVERSION RATE *(Parents of Dependent Students/Independent Students with Dependents other than a spouse)*
Asset conversion rate for Dependent Students and Independent Students without Dependents is 35%.
Asset conversion rate for Dependent Parents and Independent Students with Dependents is 12%.

INCOME ASSESSMENT RATE *(Dependent Students/Independent Students without Dependents)*
50% of available income

2004-2005 FEDERAL METHODOLOGY (FM) COMPUTATION TABLES

CONTRIBUTION FROM ADJUSTED AVAILABLE INCOME (AAI)

(Parents of Dependent Students/Independent Students with Dependents other than a spouse)

Available Income (AI)	Total Contributions from Income
Less than $ -3,409 (3,409)	$ -750
$(3,409) to 12,200	22% of AI
$12,201 to 15,400	$2,684 + 25% of AI over $12,200
$15,401 to 18,500	$3,484 + 29% of AI over $15,400
$18,501 to 21,600	$4,383 + 34% of AI over $18,500
$21,601 to 24,700	$5,437 + 40% of AI over $21,600
$24,701 or more	$6,677 + 47% of AI over $24,700

CollegeBoard

Parents of Dependent Student(s)

Student's Name:	Social Security Number:	
PARENT'S INCOME		
1. AGI/taxable income	$	
2. Total untaxed income/benefits	+	
3. Income exclusions (child support paid + education tax credits)	-	
4. Total parent's income (sum of lines 1, 2, minus line 3)	=	
ALLOWANCES		
5. U.S. income tax		
6. State and other taxes (% from Table 1 X line 4)	+	
7. F.I.C.A. (Table 2)	+	
8. Employment Allowance (Table 2)	+	
9. Income protection allowance (Table 3a)	+	
10. Total allowances (sum of lines 5 - 9)	=	
11. Available income (line 4 minus line 10)	=	
PARENT'S ASSETS		
12. Cash, savings, and checking accounts		
13. Other real estate/investment equity	+	
14. Adjusted business/farm equity (Table 4)	+	
15. Net worth (sum of lines 12 - 14)	=	
16. Asset protection allowance (Table 5)	-	
17. Discretionary net worth (line 15 minus line 16)	=	
18. Conversion percentage	X	12%
19. Income supplement (line 17 X line 118) (If simple needs test qualifier*, enter $0; if negative, enter $0)	=	
20. Adjusted available income (sum of line 11 and line 19)	=	
CONTRIBUTION**		
21. Total Contribution (calculate using line 20 and Table 8)	=	
22. Number of dependent children in college at least half time		
23. Parents' contribution for student (line 21 divided by line 22) can not be less than $0	=	

* For parents and students who file or are eligible to file IRS 1040A or 1040EZ forms or who are not required to file, no assets included in the methodology if parent's taxable income is less than $50,000
** Federal need analysis provisions provide a variant for families with parents' AGI of $15,000 or less who file or who are eligible to file the IRS 1040A or 1040EZ forms, or who are not required to file. In such cases, no contribution is expected.

Dependent Student(s)

Student's Name:	Social Security Number:	
STUDENT'S INCOME		
1. AGI/taxable income	$	
2. Untaxed income/benefits	+	
3. Taxable student aid	-	
4. Total Income (sum of lines 1 and 2, minus line 3)	=	
ALLOWANCES		
5. U.S. income tax		
6. State and other taxes (% from Table 1 X line 4)	+	
7. F.I.C.A. (Table 2)	+	
8. Income protection allowance (Table 3b)	+	
9. Parents' negative available income offset (line 11 of parents' worksheet, if negative)	+	
10. Total allowances (sum of lines 5 - 9)	=	
11. Available income (line 4 minus line 10)	=	
12. Contribution from income (line 11 X 50%); cannot be less than $0	=	
STUDENT'S ASSETS		
13. Cash, savings, and checking accounts		
14. Other real estate/investment equity	+	
15. Business/nonfamily farm equity	+	
16. Net assets (sum of lines 13 - 15)	=	
17. Contribution from assets (line 16 X .35); cannot be less than $0 (If Simple Needs Test qualifier*, enter $0)	=	
CONTRIBUTION**		
18. Total Student Contribution (sum of lines 12 and 17)	=	

* For parents and students who file or are eligible to file IRS 1040A or 1040EZ forms or who are not required to file, no assets included in the methodology if parents' taxable income is less than $50,000.
** Federal need analysis provisions provide a variant for families with parents' AGI of $15,000 or less who file or who are eligible to file the IRS 1040A or 1040EZ forms, or who are not required to file. In such cases, no contribution is expected.

Independent Student(s) With Dependent(s)

Student's Name:	**Social Security Number:**	
STUDENT'S (AND SPOUSES) INCOME		
1. AGI/taxable income	$	
2. Total untaxed income/benefits	+	
3. Income exclusions (child support paid + taxable student aid + education tax credits)	-	
4. Total Income (sum of lines 1 and 2, minus line 3)	=	
ALLOWANCES		
5. U.S. income tax		
6. State and other taxes (% from Table 1 X line 4)	+	
7. F.I.C.A. (Table 2)	+	
8. Employment Allowance (Table 2)	+	
9. Income protection allowance (Table 3a)	+	
10. Total allowances (sum of lines 5 - 9)	=	
11. Available income (line 4 minus line 10)	=	
STUDENT'S (AND SPOUSES) ASSETS		
12. Cash, savings, and checking accounts		
13. Other real estate/investment equity	+	
14. Adjusted business/nonfamily farm equity (Table 4)	+	
15. Net worth (sum of lines 12 - 14)	=	
16. Asset protection allowance (Table 5)	-	
17. Discretionary net worth (line 15 minus line 16)	=	
18. Conversion percentage	X	12%
19. Income supplement (line 17 X line 118) (If simple needs test qualifier*, enter $0; if negative, enter $0)	=	
20. Adjusted available income (sum of lines 11 and line 19)	=	
CONTRIBUTION**		
21. Total Student's Contribution (calculate using line 20 and Table 8)	=	
22. Number of family members enrolled at least half time		
23. Contribution for student (line 21 divided by line 22; if negative, enter zero)	=	

* For parents and students who file or are eligible to file IRS 1040A or 1040EZ forms or who are not required to file, no assets included in the methodology if parents' taxable income is less than $50,000
** Federal need analysis provisions provide a variant for families with parents' AGI of $15,000 or less who file or who are eligible to file the IRS 1040A or 1040EZ forms, or who are not required to file. In such cases, no contribution is expected.

Independent Student(s) Without Dependent(s)

Student's Name:	Social Security Number:	
STUDENT'S (AND SPOUSES) INCOME		
1. AGI/taxable income		S
2. Total untaxed income/benefits		+
3. Income exclusions (child support paid + taxable student aid + education tax credits)		-
4. Total Income (sum of lines 1 and 2, minus line 3)		=
ALLOWANCES		
5. U.S. income tax		
6. State and other taxes (% from Table 1 X line 4)		+
7. F.I.C.A. (Table 2)		+
8. Employment Allowance (Table 2)		+
9. Income protection allowance (Table 3b)		+
10. Total allowances (sum of lines 5 - 9)		=
11. Available income (line 4 minus line 10)		=
12. Student's contribution from income (line 11 X 50%)		
STUDENT'S (AND SPOUSES) ASSETS		
13. Cash, savings, and checking accounts		
14. Other real estate/investment equity		+
15. Adjusted business/nonfamily farm equity (Table 4)		+
16. Net worth (sum of lines 13 - 15)		=
17. Asset protection allowance (Table 5)		-
18. Discretionary net worth (line 16 minus line 17)		=
19. Student's contribution from assets (line 18 times 35%) **(If simple needs test qualifier*, enter $0; if negative, enter $0)**		=
CONTRIBUTION**		
20. Total Student's Contribution **(sum of lines 12 and 19, divided by 2 if spouse is enrolled; if negative, enter zero)**		=

* For students who file or are eligible to file IRS 1040A or 1040EZ forms or who aren't required to file, no assets included in the methodology if student's taxable income is less than $50,000
** Federal need analysis provisions provide a variant for families with parents' AGI of $15,000 or less who file or who are eligible to file the IRS 1040A or 1040EZ forms, or who are not required to file. In such cases, no contribution is expected.

ALLOWANCES FOR STATE AND OTHER TAXES									
	Parents of Dependent Students							Students	
	Total Income							Taxable Income	
State/Territory/Country of Residence	$0–30,000	$30,001–40,000	$40,001–50,000	$50,001–60,000	$60,001–70,000	$70,001–80,000	$80,001–90,000	$0–20,000	$20,001–or more
Alabama (AL)	9.0%	8.5%	8.0%	7.5%	7.0%	6.5%	6.5%	2.5%	3.0%
Alaska (AK)	4.5	4.0	3.5	3.0	2.5	2.0	2.0	0.0	0.0
American Samoa (AS)	4.5	4.0	3.5	3.0	2.5	2.0	2.0	0.0	0.0
Arizona (AZ)	8.0	7.5	7.0	7.0	7.0	6.5	6.5	0.5	1.0
Arkansas (AR)	9.0	8.5	8.0	8.0	8.0	8.0	8.0	1.5	2.0
California (CA)	8.0	8.0	7.5	7.5	8.0	8.0	8.0	0.5	1.0
Canada (CN)	4.5	4.0	3.5	3.0	2.5	2.0	2.0	4.0	5.0
Colorado (CO)	8.0	8.0	7.5	7.5	7.5	7.5	7.0	1.5	2.0
Connecticut (CT)	10.0	9.5	9.0	9.0	9.5	9.5	9.5	0.5	1.0
Delaware (DE)	6.0	6.0	6.0	6.0	6.5	7.0	7.0	2.5	3.0
District of Columbia (DC)	8.5	8.5	8.5	9.0	9.0	9.0	9.0	3.5	4.0
Federated States of Micronesia (FM)	4.5	4.0	3.5	3.0	2.5	2.0	2.0	0.0	0.0
Florida (FL)	7.5	7.0	6.5	6.0	5.5	5.0	4.5	0.0	0.0
Georgia (GA)	9.0	8.5	8.5	8.5	8.0	8.0	8.0	1.5	2.0
Guam (GU)	4.5	4.0	3.5	3.0	2.5	2.0	2.0	0.0	0.0
Hawaii (HI)	9.0	9.0	9.0	9.0	8.5	8.5	8.5	3.0	3.5
Idaho (ID)	8.5	8.5	8.5	8.5	8.5	8.5	8.5	1.0	1.5
Illinois (IL)	10.0	9.5	9.0	8.5	8.0	8.0	7.5	1.5	2.0
Indiana (IN)	9.5	9.0	8.5	8.0	7.5	7.5	7.5	2.5	3.0
Iowa (IA)	10.0	10.5	9.0	9.0	9.0	9.0	9.0	2.0	2.5
Kansas (KS)	9.0	8.5	8.5	8.5	8.5	8.0	8.0	1.5	2.0
Kentucky (KY)	9.5	9.5	9.5	9.5	9.5	9.5	9.5	3.0	3.5
Louisiana (LA)	9.0	8.5	8.0	7.5	7.0	7.0	6.5	1.0	1.5
Maine (ME)	9.0	9.0	9.0	9.5	9.5	9.5	9.5	1.0	1.5
Marshall Islands (MH)	4.5	4.0	3.5	3.0	2.5	2.0	2.0	0.0	0.0
Maryland (MD)	11.0	10.5	10.5	10.5	10.5	10.5	10.5	3.5	4.0

ALLOWANCES FOR STATE AND OTHER TAXES								
	Parents of Dependent Students							*Students*
	Total Income							**Taxable Income**
State/Territory/Country of Residence	$0–30,000	$30,001–40,000	$40,001–50,000	$50,001–60,000	$60,001–70,000	$70,001–80,000	$80,001–90,000	$0–20,000	$20,001–or more
Massachusetts (MA)	10.5	10.0	9.5	9.5	9.5	9.5	9.5	3.0	3.5
Mexico (MX)	4.5	4.0	3.5	3.0	2.5	2.0	2.0	4.0	5.0
Michigan (MI)	11.0	10.5	10.0	9.5	9.0	9.0	8.5	2.5	3.0
Minnesota (MN)	9.0	9.0	9.0	9.0	9.0	9.0	9.0	1.5	2.0
Mississippi	8.0	8.0	8.0	8.0	8.0	7.5	7.0	0.5	1.0
Missouri (MO)	9.0	9.0	9.0	8.5	8.5	8.5	8.0	2.0	2.5
Montana (MT)	6.0	6.0	6.0	6.0	6.5	6.5	6.5	1.5	2.0
Nebraska (NE)	9.0	9.0	9.0	9.0	9.0	9.0	9.0	1.0	1.5
Nevada (NV)	6.0	5.5	5.0	4.5	4.0	3.5	3.5	0.0	0.0
New Hampshire (NH)	7.5	7.0	6.5	6.0	5.5	5.5	5.5	0.0	0.0
New Jersey (NJ)	12.0	11.5	11.0	10.5	10.0	9.5	9.0	1.0	1.5
New Mexico (NM)	9.0	9.0	8.5	8.5	8.0	8.0	8.0	0.5	1.0
New York (NY)	12.5	12.5	12.5	12.5	12.5	12.5	12.5	1.5	2.0
North Carolina (NC)	8.5	8.5	8.5	8.5	8.5	8.5	8.5	1.5	2.0
North Dakota (ND)	7.5	7.0	6.5	6.5	6.5	6.0	6.0	0.5	1.0
Northern Mariana Islands (NP)	4.5	4.0	3.5	3.0	2.5	2.0	2.0	0.0	0.0
Ohio (OH)	9.5	9.0	9.0	9.0	9.0	9.0	9.0	2.5	3.0
Oklahoma (OK)	8.5	8.5	8.5	8.5	8.0	8.0	8.0	1.0	1.5
Oregon (OR)	9.5	9.5	9.5	10.0	10.0	10.0	10.0	3.0	3.5
Palau (PW)	4.5	4.0	3.5	3.0	2.5	2.0	2.0	0.0	0.0
Pennsylvania (PA)	10.5	10.0	9.5	9.0	9.0	8.5	8.5	2.5	3.0
Puerto Rico (PR)	4.5	4.0	3.5	3.0	2.5	2.0	2.0	1.0	1.0
Rhode Island (RI)	10.5	10.0	9.5	9.5	9.5	9.5	9.5	1.0	1.5
South Carolina (SC)	6.5	6.5	7.0	7.5	7.5	7.5	7.5	0.5	1.0
South Dakota (SD)	7.5	7.0	6.5	6.0	5.5	5.0	5.0	0.0	0.0
Tennessee (TN)	7.5	7.0	6.5	6.0	5.5	5.0	4.5	0.0	0.0

ALLOWANCES FOR STATE AND OTHER TAXES								
	Parents of Dependent Students						Students	
	Total Income						Taxable Income	
State/Territory/Country of Residence	$0-30,000	$30,001-40,000	$40,001-50,000	$50,001-60,000	$60,001-70,000	$70,001-80,000	$80,001-90,000	$0-20,000	$20,001-or more
Texas (TX)	7.5	7.0	6.5	6.0	5.5	5.5	5.0	0.0	0.0
Utah (UT)	10.0	10.0	10.0	9.5	9.0	9.0	8.5	1.5	2.0
Vermont (VT)	8.0	8.0	8.0	8.0	8.0	8.0	8.0	0.5	1.0
Virgin Islands (VI)	4.5	4.0	3.5	3.0	2.5	2.0	2.0	0.0	0.0
Virginia (VA)	8.0	8.0	8.0	8.0	8.0	8.0	8.0	2.0	2.5
Washington (WA)	10.0	9.5	9.0	8.5	8.0	7.5	7.0	0.0	0.0
West Virginia (WV)	8.0	7.5	7.5	7.5	7.5	7.5	7.5	2.0	2.5
Wisconsin (WI)	11.5	11.5	11.5	11.5	11.5	11.0	10.5	1.5	2.0
Wyoming (WY)	5.5	5.0	4.0	4.0	4.0	4.5	3.0	0.0	0.0
Not Reported (NR)	9.5	9.0	8.5	8.5	8.0	8.0	8.0	1.5	2.0

2004–2005 Institutional Methodology (IM) Computation Tables
continued

ALLOWANCES AGAINST INCOME	
FICA: Wages	
$1 to $87,000	7.65% of income earned by each wage earner (maximum $6,655.50 per person)
$87,001 or more	$6,655.50 + 1.45% of income earned above $87,000 by each wage earner
Elementary/secondary tuition allowance	Reported tuition paid to maximum $7,655 per eligible child
Employment allowance	40% of lesser earned income to a maximum of $3,620 (single parent: 40% of earned income to a maximum of $3,620)
Medical/dental expense allowance	Un-reimbursed expenses in excess of 3.4% of total income

INCOME PROTECTION ALLOWANCE (IPA) *(Parents of Dependent Students)*					
Family Size* (including student)	Number in College**				
	1	2	3	4	5
2	$17,580	$16,930			
3	$21,250	$20,600	$19,950		
4	$24,420	$23,770	$23,120	$22,470	
5	$27,350	$26,700	$26,050	$25,400	$24,750
6	$29,790	$29,140	$28,490	$27,840	$27,190

* For each additional family member, add $2,440.
** For each additional college student, subtract $650

ADJUSTED NET WORTH OF A BUSINESS OR FARM	
Net Worth (NW)	Adjusted Net Worth
Less than $1	$0
$1 to 100,000	$0 + 40% of NW
$100,001 to 295,000	$40,000 + 50% of NW over $100,000
$295,001 to $490,000	$137,500 + 60% of NW over $295,000
$490,001 or more	$254,500 + 100% of NW over $490,000

EDUCATION SAVINGS ALLOWANCE

Annual Savings Goal (ASG) =
1.52% of Total Income, to a maximum of $2,050

Annual Education Savings Allowance (AESA) =
ASG x number of pre-college children, excluding the student applicant

Cumulative Education Savings Allowance (CESA) =
[(Number of college students x ASG x 18 x .625) +
(ASG x total ages of pre-college children)] OR $17,330, whichever is greater*

*Minimum CESA applies to parents of dependent students only

CONTRIBUTION FROM AVAILABLE INCOME (AI)
(Parents of Dependent Students)

Available Income (AI)	Total Contributions from Income
Less than $14,000	22% of AI
$14,001 to 18,900	$3,080 + 26% of AI over $14,000
$18,901 to 23,800	$4354 + 30% of AI over $18,900
$23,801 to 28,700	$5,824 + 34% of AI over $23,800
$28,701 to 33,600	$7,490 + 38% of AI over $28,700
$33,601 to 38,500	$9352 + 42% of AI over $33,600
$38,501 or more	$11,410 + 46 %of AI over $38,500

STUDENT INCOME ASSESSMENT RATES

Dependent Students	50% of Available Income (AI)
Independent Students	70% of Available Income (AI)

ADJUSTED NET WORTH OF A BUSINESS OR FARM

Net Worth (NW)	Adjusted Net Worth
Less than $1	$0
$1 to $100,000	$0 + 40% of NW
$100,001 to 295,000	$40,000 + 50% of NW over $100,000
$295,001 to 490,000	$137,500 + 60% of NW over $295,000
$490,001 or more	$254,500 + 100% of NW over $490,000

EMERGENCY RESERVE ALLOWANCE (ERA)

Parents of Dependents and Independents Students with Dependents:

Family Size	ERA
2	$15,960
3	$19,280
4	$22,170
5	$24,830
6	$27,040
Each additional family member	+$2,210
Single Independent Students without Dependents	$1,560
Married Independent Students without Dependents	$2,240

ASSET CONVERSION RATE

Parents of Dependents Students

Discretionary Net Worth	Total Contribution From Assets
Up to $27,040	3%
27,041 to 54,080	$810 + 4% of DNW over $27,040
54,081 or more	$1,890 + 5% of DNV over $54,080
All students: Asset conversion rate is 25% of discretionary net worth	

| NUMBER IN COLLEGE ADJUSTMENT ||
Number of Children in College	Adjustment Rate
1	100% of PC
2	60%
3	45%
4 or more	35%

For independent students, the adjustment rate is determined by the total number in college, including the student, spouse, and dependent children.

STUDENT MINIMUM STANDARD CONTRIBUTION	
$1,150	Freshman Dependent Students
$1,400	All Other Dependent Students
$1,900	All Independent Students

CollegeBoard

Parents of Dependent Student(s)

Student's Name:	Social Security Number:	
INCOME OF PARENT(S)		
1. AGI/taxable income		$
a. Add back losses from business, farm, etc., and capital losses		+
2. Untaxed income & benefits		+
3. Child support paid		−
4. Total parent's income (sum of lines 1, 1a, 2, minus 3)		=
ALLOWANCES		
5. U.S. income tax		
6. State and other taxes (% from Table 1 X line 4)		+
7. F.I.C.A. (Table 2)		+
8. Medical/dental expense allowance (Table 2)		+
9. Employment allowance (Table 2)		+
10. Annual education savings allowance (AESA) (Table 4):		
a. Annual savings goal (1.52% X line 4, up to $2,050)	=	
b. Number of pre-college children, excluding student	=	
c. Total AESA (line 10a X 10b)		+
11. Income protection allowance (Table 3a)		+
12. Total allowances (sum of lines 5 - 11)		=
13. Available income (line 4 minus line 12)		=
14. Total PC from income (calculate using line 13 and Table 5 - may not be negative)		=
ASSETS		
15. Cash, savings, and checking accounts		
16. Home equity		+
17. Investment equity		+
18. Other real estate equity		+
19. Adjusted business/farm equity (Table 7)		+

20. Assets in siblings' names/Prepaid tuition plans:			
a. Parents' assets held in names of siblings	+		
b. Prepaid tuition plan assets for siblings	+		
c. Prepaid tuition plan assets for students	+		
d. Total assets in siblings' name/Prepaid tuition plans (sum of a + b + c)		+	
21. Net worth (sum of lines 15 - 20d)		=	
22. Asset protection allowances:			
a. Emergency reserve allowance (Table 8)	=		
b. Cumulative education savings allowance (CESA) (Table 4)	=		
c. Low income asset allowance (amount from line 13, if negative)	=		
d. Total asset allowances (sum of a + b +c)		-	
23. Discretionary net worth (line 21 minus line 22d - may not be negative)		=	
24. Total PC from assets (calculate using line 23 and Table 9)		=	
CONTRIBUTION			
25. Total parent contribution (sum of line 14 and line 24)		=	
26. Number in college adjustment (Table 10)		X	%
27. Parent contribution for student (line 25 X line 26)		=	

2004-2005 INSTITUTIONAL METHODOLOGY (IM) WORKSHEET

Independent Student(s)

Student's Name:	Social Security Number:	
INCOME OF STUDENT (& SPOUSE)		
1. AGI/taxable income		$
2. Untaxed income/benefits		+
3. Income adjustments (child support paid + taxable student aid)		-
4. Total family income (sum of lines 1 and 2, minus 3)		=
ALLOWANCES		
5. U.S. income tax		
6. State and other taxes (% from Table 1 X line 1)		+
7. F.I.C.A. (Table 2)		+
8. Medical/dental expense allowance (Table 2)		+
9. Employment Allowance (Table 2)		+
10. Annual education savings allowance (AESA) (Table 4):		
a. Annual savings goal (1.52% X line 4, up to $2,050)	=	
b. Number of pre-college children	=	
c. Total AESA (line 10a X 10b)		+
11. Income protection allowance (Table 3b)		+
12. Total allowances (sum of lines 5 - 11)		=
13. Available income (line 4 minus line 12)		=
14. SC from income [(line 13 X 70%) X number in college adjustment (Table 10)] or minimum student contribution (Table 11), whichever is greater		=
ASSETS		
15. Cash, savings, and checking accounts		
16. Home equity		+
17. Investment equity		+
18. Other real estate equity		+
19. Adjusted business/farm equity (Table 7)		+
20. Value of trusts		+
21. Net worth (sum of lines 15 - 20)		=

22. Asset protection allowances:		
a. Emergency reserve allowance (Table 8):	=	
b. Cumulative education savings allowance (CESA) (Table 4. dependent children only)	=	
c. Total asset allowance (Sum of a + b)		-
23. Discretionary net worth (line 21 minus line 22c - may not be negative)		=
24. Total SC from assets (line 23 X .25)		=
25. SC from assets [line 24 X number in college adjustment (Table 10)]		=
CONTRIBUTION		
26. Total contribution (sum of line 14 and line 25)		=

2004-2005 INSTITUTIONAL METHODOLOGY (IM) WORKSHEET

Dependent Student

Student's Name:	Social Security Number:
INCOME OF STUDENT	
1. AGI/taxable income	$
2. Total untaxed income/benefits	+
3. Taxable student aid	-
4. Total income (sum of lines 1, 2, minus line 3)	=
ALLOWANCES	
5. U.S. income tax	
6. State and other taxes (% from Table 1 X line 1)	+
7. F.I.C.A. (Table 2)	+
8. Total allowances (sum of lines 5 - 7)	=
9. Available income (line 4 minus line 8)	=
10. SC from income (line 9 X 50%) or minimum student contribution (Table 11), whichever is greater	=
ASSETS	
12. Cash, savings, and checking accounts	
12. Home equity	+
13. Investment equity	+
14. Other real estate equity	+
15. Business/farm equity	+
16. Trust value	+
17. Net worth (sum of lines 11 - 16	=
18. SC from assets (line 17 X .25)	=
CONTRIBUTION	
19. Total student contribution (sum of line 10 and line 18)	=

APPENDIX G

STATE GRANT, SCHOLARSHIP, AND GUARANTY AGENCIES

ALABAMA

LEAPP
Alabama Commission on Higher
    Education
PO Box 302000
Montgomery, AL 36130-2000
334-242-1998

Byrd
State Department of Education
Gordon Persons Office Building
PO Box 302101
Montgomery, AL 36130-2010
334-242-8059

Guaranty Agency
Kentucky Higher Education Assistance
    Authority
1050 U S 127 South
Suite 102
Frankfort, KY 40601-4323
502-696-7200, 800-928-8926
webmaster@kheaa.com

ALASKA

LEAPP State Guaranty Agency
(State Loans)
Alaska Commission on Postsecondary
    Education
3030 Vintage Boulevard
Juneau, AK 99801
907-465-2962, 800-441-2962

Byrd
State Department of Education
Goldbelt Place
801 West 10th St., Suite 200
Juneau, AK 99801-1894
907-465-2800

Federal Guaranty Agency
(Federal Loans)
Sallie Mae
PO Box 6180
Indianapolis, IN 46206
317-849-6510, 800-428-9250

ARIZONA

LEAPP
Arizona Commission for
    Postsecondary Education
2020 N. Central Avenue
Suite 550
Phoenix, AZ 85004-4503
602-258-2435

Byrd
State Department of Education
1535 West Jefferson
Phoenix, AZ 85007
602-542-7469

Guaranty Agency
Sallie Mae
PO Box 6180
Indianapolis, IN 46206
317-849-6510, 800-428-9250

ARKANSAS

LEAPP
Arkansas Dept of Higher Education
114 East Capitol
Little Rock, AR 72201-3818
501-371-2000

Byrd
Arkansas Department of Education
4 State Capitol Mall
Room 107A
Little Rock, AR 72201-1071
501-682-4396

Guaranty Agency
Student Loan Guarantee Foundation
219 South Victory Street
Little Rock, AR 72201-1884
501-372-1491, 800-622-3446

CALIFORNIA
LEAPP, Byrd, Guaranty Agency
California Student Aid Commission
PO Box 419026
Rancho Cordova, CA 95741-9026
916-526-7590, 800-367-1589

COLORADO
LEAPP
Colorado Commission on
Higher Education
1380 Lawrence Street
Suite 1200
Denver, CO 80204
303-866-2723

Byrd
U.S. Department of Education
201 East Colfax Avenue
Denver, CO 80203
303-866-6600

Guaranty Agency
Colorado Guaranteed
Student Loan Program
999 18th Street
Suite 425
Denver, CO 80202-2471
303-305-3000, 800-727-9834

CONNECTICUT
LEAPP, Byrd
Connecticut Dept of Higher Education
61 Woodland Street
Hartford, CT 06105-2326
860-947-1800

Guaranty Agency
Connecticut Student Loan Foundation
525 Brook Street
Rocky Hill, CT 06067
860-257-4001, 800-237-9721

DELAWARE
LEAPP
Delaware Higher Education
Commission
Carvel State Office Building
820 North French Street
Wilmington, DE 19801
302-577-3240

Byrd
Delaware Department of Education
Townsend Building
Federal and Lockerman Streets
PO Box 1402
Dover, DE 19903-1402
302-739-5622

Guaranty Agency
Pennsylvania Higher Education
Assistance Agency
1200 North Seventh Street
Harrisburg, PA 17102-1444
717-720-2860, 800-692-7392

DISTRICT OF COLUMBIA
LEAPP
Department of Human Services
Office of Postsecondary Education,
Research and Assistance
2100 Martin Luther King, Jr. Ave. S.E.
Suite 401
Washington, DC 20020
202-698-2400
Byrd
District of Columbia Public Schools
Division of Student Services
825 North Capitol Street, NE
Washington, DC 20019
202-442-5110

DC Tuition Assistance Program
441 4th Street, NW
Suite 400
Washington, DC 20001
202-727-2824

Guaranty Agency
American Student Assistance
330 Stuart Street
Boston, MA 02116-5292
617-426-9434, 800-999-9080

FLORIDA

LEAPP, Byrd, Guaranty Agency
Florida Department of Education
Office of Student Financial —
   State/Federal Programs
124 Collins Building
325 W. Gaines Street
Tallahassee, FL 32399-0400
850-410-5190 (LEAPP)
850-410-5180 (Byrd)
850-410-5200, 800-366-3475
   (Guaranty Agency)

GEORGIA

LEAPP Hope Scholarship,
Guaranty Agency
Georgia Student Finance Commission
State Loans and Grants Division
2082 East Exchange Place
Suite 220
Tucker, GA 30084
770-724-9000

Byrd
State Department of Education
Twin Towers East
17th Floor
205 Butler Street
Atlanta, GA 30334
404-657-0183

HAWAII

LEAPP
Hawaii State Postsecondary Education
   Commission
2444 Dole Street
Room 209
Honolulu, HI 96822-2302
808-956-8213

Byrd
Hawaii Department of Education
641 18th Avenue
Building V
Room 201
Honolulu, HI 96816-4444
808-735-6222

Guaranty Agency
Sallie Mae
PO Box 6180
Indianapolis, IN 46206
317-849-6510, 800-428-9250

IDAHO

LEAPP
Idaho State Board of Education
PO Box 83720
Boise, ID 83720-0027
208-334-2270

Byrd
State Department of Education
650 W. State Street
Boise, ID 83720-0027
208-332-6800

Guaranty Agency
Northwest Education Loan Association
500 Coleman Building
811 First Avenue
Seattle, WA 98104
206-461-5300, 800-562-3001

ILLINOIS

LEAPP, Byrd, Guaranty Agency
Illinois Student Assistance
 Commission
1755 Lake Cook Road
Deerfield, IL 60015-5209
847-948-8500 (LEAPP, Byrd)
847-948-8500, 800-899-4722
 (Guaranty Agency)

INDIANA

LEAPP, Byrd
State Student Assistance Commission
 of Indiana
Student Assistance
150 West Market Street
Suite 500
Indianapolis, IN 46204-2811
317-232-2350

Guaranty Agency
Sallie Mae
PO Box 6180
Indianapolis, IN 46206
317-849-6510, 800-428-9250

IOWA

LEAPP, Byrd, Guaranty Agency
Iowa College Student Aid Commission
200 Tenth Street
4th Floor
Des Moines, IA 50309-3609
515-281-3501, 800-383-4222

KANSAS

LEAPP
Kansas Board of Regents
700 S.W. Harrison
Suite 1410
Topeka, KS 66603-3760
785-296-3517

Byrd
State Department of Education
Kansas State Education Building
120 East South 10th Avenue
Topeka, KS 66612-1103
785-296-4950

Guaranty Agency
Sallie Mae
PO Box 6180
Indianapolis, IN 46206
317-849-6510, 800-428-9250

KENTUCKY

LEAPP, Guaranty Agency
Kentucky Higher Education Assistance
 Authority
1050 U.S. 127 South
Frankfort, KY 40601-4323
502-696-7200, 800-928-8926
www.kheaa.com

Byrd
State Department of Education
500 Mero Street
1919 Capital Plaza Tower
Frankfort, KY 40601
502-564-3421

LOUISIANA

LEAPP, Guaranty Agency
Louisiana Student Financial Assistance
 Commission
PO Box 91202
Baton Rouge, LA 70821-9202
225-922-1011, 800-259-5626

Byrd
State Department of Education
626 North 4th Street
12th Floor
PO Box 94064
Baton Rouge, LA 70804-9064
225-342-2098

MAINE

LEAPP, Byrd, Guaranty Agency
Maine Education Assistance Division
Finance Authority of Maine
5 Community Drive
PO Box 949
Augusta, ME 04332-0949
Education Assistance Division
207 623-3263, 207-626-8200 (LEAPP)
207-287-2183 (Byrd)
207-623-3263, 800-228-3734
  (Guaranty Agency)

MARYLAND

LEAPP, HOPE Scholarship
Maryland Higher Education
  Commission
Jeffrey Building
16 Francis Street
Annapolis, MD 21401-1781
410-260-4565

Byrd
Maryland State Dept of Education
200 West Baltimore Street
Baltimore, MD 21201-2595
410-767-0480

MASSACHUSETTS

LEAPP
Massachusetts Higher Education
  Coordinating Council
330 Stuart Street
Boston, MA 02116-5251
617-727-9420

Byrd
State Department of Education
350 Main Street
Malden, MA 02148-5023
781-338-3300

Guaranty Agency
American Student Assistance
330 Stuart Street
Boston, MA 02116-5292
617-426-9434, 800-999-9080

MICHIGAN

LEAPP
Michigan Higher Education Assistance
  Authority
Office of Scholarships and Grants
PO Box 30462
Lansing, MI 48909-7962
517-373-3394

Byrd
State Department of Treasury
PO Box 30008
608 West Allegan Street
Lansing, MI 48909
517-373-3394, 888-447-2687

Guaranty Agency
Michigan Higher Education Assistance
  Authority
Office of Michigan Guaranty Agency
PO Box 30047
Lansing, MI 48909-7547
517-373-0760, 800-642-5626

MINNESOTA

LEAPP
Minnesota Higher Education
Services Office
14500 Energy Park Drive
Suite 350
St. Paul, MN 55108-5277
800-657-3866
Byrd
State Department of Education
712 Capitol Square Building
550 Cedar Street
St. Paul, MN 55101
651-582-8280

Guaranty Agency
Great Lakes Higher Education
PO Box 7658
2401 International Lane
Madison, WI 53704
608-246-1800, 800-236-5900

MISSISSIPPI

LEAPP
Mississippi Postsecondary Education
   Financial Assistance Board
3825 Ridgewood Road
Jackson, MS 39211-6453
601-432-6663

Byrd
State Department of Education
PO Box 771
550 High Street
Room 501
Jackson, MS 39205-0771
601-359-3513

MISSOURI

LEAPP, Guaranty Agency
Missouri Coordinating Board for
   Higher Education
3515 Amazonas Drive
Jefferson City, MO 65109-5717
573-751-2361 (LEAPP)
573-751-3940, 800-473-6757
   (Guaranty Agency)

Byrd
State Department of Elementary and
   Secondary Education
PO Box 480
205 Jefferson Street
7th floor
Jefferson City, MO 65102-0480
573-751-1668

MONTANA

LEAPP
Montana University System
2500 Broadway
PO Box 203101
Helena, MT 59620-3101
406-444-6570

Byrd
State Office of Public Instruction
PO Box 202501
Helena, MT 59620-2501
406-444-4422

Guaranty Agency
Montana Guaranteed Student Loan
   Program
2500 Broadway
PO Box 203101
Helena, MT 59620-3101
406-444-6594, 800-537-7508

NEBRASKA

LEAPP
Coordinating Commission for
   Postsecondary Education
PO Box 95005
140 N. 8th Street
Suite 300
Lincoln, NE 68509-5005
402-471-2847

Byrd
Nebraska Department of Education
PO Box 94987
301 Centennial Mall South
Lincoln, NE 68509-4987
402-471-2847

Guaranty Agency
Nebraska Student Loan Program
PO Box 82507
Lincoln, NE 68501-2507
402-475-8686, 800-735-8778

NEVADA

LEAPP, Byrd
Nevada Department of Education
700 East Fifth Street
Carson City, NV 89701-5096
775-687-9200 (LAAP)
702-687-9228 (Byrd)

Guaranty Agency
Sallie Mae
PO Box 6180
Indianapolis, IN 46206
317-849-6510, 800-428-9250

NEW HAMPSHIRE

LEAPP
New Hampshire Postsecondary
    Education Commission
2 Industrial Park Drive
Concord, NH 03301-8512
603-271-2555

Byrd
State Department of Education
State Office Park South
101 Pleasant Street
Concord, NH 03301-3860
603-271-6051

Guaranty Agency
New Hampshire Higher Education
    Assistance Foundation
PO Box 877
4 Barrell Court
Concord, NH 03302-0877
603-225-6612, 800-525-2577

NEW JERSEY

LEAPP
State of New Jersey
Office of Student Financial Assistance
4 Quakerbridge Plaza
CN 540
Trenton, NJ 08625
800-792-8670

Byrd
State Department of Education
PO Box 500
Trenton, NJ 08625-0500
609-984-6314

Guaranty Agency
Office of Student Assistance
4 Quakerbridge Plaza
CN 543
Trenton, NJ 08625-0540
609-588-3214, 800-792-8670

NEW MEXICO

LEAPP
New Mexico Commission on
Higher Education
1068 Cerrillos Road
Santa Fe, NM 87501
505-827-7396

Byrd
State Department of Education
Education Building
300 Don Gaspar
Santa Fe, NM 87501-2786
505-827-6648

Guaranty Agency
New Mexico Student Loan Program
3900 Osuna NE
Albuquerque, NM 87199-2230
505-345-8821, 800-279-3070

NEW YORK

LEAPP
New York State Higher Education
    Services Corporation
One Commerce Plaza
Albany, NY 12255
888-697-4372

Guaranty Agency
New York State Higher Education
   Services Corporation
99 Washington Avenue
Albany, NY 12255
518-473-7087, 888-697-4372

NORTH CAROLINA
LEAPP, Guaranty Agency
North Carolina State Education
   Assistance Authority
10 Alexander Drive
PO Box 13663
Research Triangle Park, NC 27709
919-549-8614, 800-700-1775
   (Guarantee Agency)

Byrd
State Department of Public Instruction
Education Building
Division of Teacher Education
301 North Wilmington Street
Raleigh, NC 27601
919-807-3369

NORTH DAKOTA
LEAPP
North Dakota University System
North Dakota Student Financial
   Assistance Program
600 East Boulevard-D215
Bismarck, ND 58505-0230
701-328-4114

Byrd
State Dept. of Public Instruction
State Capitol Building
11th floor
600 East Boulevard Avenue
Bismarck, ND 58505-0440
701-328-2317

Guaranty Agency
Student Loans of North Dakota
Bank of North Dakota
PO Box 5524
Bismarck, ND 58506-5524
701-328-5754, 800-472-2166

OHIO
LEAPP
Ohio Board of Regents
88 East Broad Street
Suite 350
Columbus, OH 43215
614-466-7420, 614-752-9488

Byrd
State Department of Education
65 South Front Street
Room 1009
Columbus, OH 43266-0308
614-466-2761 (Byrd)

Guaranty Agency
Great Lakes Higher Education
   Guaranty Corporation
PO Box 7658
2401 International Lane
Madison WI 53707-7858
608-246-1800, 800-236-5900

OKLAHOMA
LEAPP, Guaranty Agency
Oklahoma State Regents for
Higher Education
Oklahoma Tuition Aid Grant Program
PO Box 3000
Oklahoma City, OK 73101-3000
405-234-4300, 800-442-8642

Byrd
State Department of Education
Oliver Hodge Memorial
Education Building
2500 North Lincoln Boulevard
Oklahoma City, OK 73105-4599
405-521-3301

OREGON

LEAPP, Byrd, Guaranty Agency
Oregon Student Assistance
    Commission
1500 Valley River Drive
Suite 100
Eugene, OR 97401
541-687-7375 (LEAPP, Byrd)
800-452-8807 (Guaranty Agency)

PENNSYLVANIA

LEAPP, Byrd, Guaranty Agency
Pennsylvania Higher Education
    Assistance Agency
1200 North 7th Street
Harrisburg, PA 17102-1444
717-720-2860
800-692-7392 (Guaranty Agency)

RHODE ISLAND

LEAPP, Guaranty Agency
Rhode Island Higher Education
    Assistance Authority
560 Jefferson Boulevard
Warwick, RI 02886
401-736-1100, 800-922-9855
Byrd
State Department of Education
255 Westminister Street
Providence, RI 02903
401-222-4600, x2194

SOUTH CAROLINA

LEAPP
South Carolina Higher Education
    Tuition Grants Commission
101 Business Park Boulevard
Suite 2100
Columbia, SC 29203
803-896-1120

Byrd
State Department of Education
605-a Rutledge Building
1429 Senate Street
Columbia, SC 29201
803-734-8116

Guaranty Agency
South Carolina Student Loan Corp.
PO Box 210219
Suite 200, Interstate Center
Columbia, SC 29221
803-798-0916, 800-347-2752

SOUTH DAKOTA

LEAPP, Byrd
Department of
Education and Cultural Affairs
700 Governors Drive
Pierre, SD 57501-2291
605-773-3134

Guaranty Agency
Education Assistance Corporation
115 First Avenue S.W.
Aberdeen, SD 57401-4174
605-225-6423, 800-592-1802

TENNESSEE

LEAPP, Byrd, Guaranty Agency
Tennessee Student
Assistance Corporation
404 James Robertson Parkway
Parkway Towers
Suite 1950
Nashville, TN 37243-0820
615-741-1346
800-342-1663 (Tenn. Residents only)

Byrd
State Department of Education
710 James Robertson Parkway
Andrew Johnson Towers, 6th Floor
Nashville, TN 37243-0375
615-741-2731
800-342-1663 (Tenn. Residents only)

TEXAS

LEAPP
Texas Higher Education Coordinating
 Board
1200 East Anderson Lane
Austin, TX 78711
800-242-3062

Byrd
Texas Education Agency
William B. Travis Building
1701 N. Congress Avenue
Austin, TX 78701
512-463-9734

Guaranty Agency
Texas Guaranteed Student Loan
 Corporation
PO Box 201725
Austin, TX 78720-1725
512-219-5700, 800-845-6267

UTAH

LEAPP, Guarantee Agency
Utah Higher Education
Assistance Authority
355 West North Temple
#3 Triad Center
Suite 550
Salt Lake City, UT 84180-1205
801-325-7206 (LEAPP)
801-321-7200, 800-418-8757
 (Guaranty Agency)

Byrd
Utah State Office of Education
250 East 500 South
Salt Lake City, UT 84111
801-538-7779

VERMONT

LEAPP, Byrd, Guaranty Agency
Vermont Student Assistance Corp.
PO Box 2000
Champlain Mill
Winooski, VT 05404-2601
800-642-3177
802-655-9602 (Byrd)
800-798-8722 (Guaranty Agency outside Vermont)

VIRGINIA

LEAPP, Byrd
State Council of Higher Education for
 Virginia
James Monroe Building
101 North 14th Street
Richmond, VA 23218-2120
804-786-1690 (LEAPP)
804-225-2877 (Byrd)

Guaranty Agency
Education Credit Management
 Corporation (Virginia)
Boulder VII
Suite 200
7325 Boufant Springs Drive
Richmond, VA 23225
804-267-7100, 888-775-3262

WASHINGTON

LEAPP
Washington State Higher Education
 Coordinating Board
917 Lakeridge Way S.W.
PO Box 43430
Olympia, WA 98504-3430
360-725-6025 (LEAPP)

Byrd
State Department of Public Instruction
PO Box 47200
Olympia, WA 98504-3211
360-753-2858

Guaranty Agency
Northwest Education Loan Association
500 Coleman Building,
811 First Avenue
Seattle, WA 98104
206-461-5300, 800-562-3001

WEST VIRGINIA

LEAPP
State College and University Systems
   of West Virginia, Central
Office
1018 Kanawha Blvd East
Suite 700
Charleston, WV 25301
304-558-4614

Byrd
State Department of Education
1900 Canal Boulevard East,
Building 6
Room 358
Charleston, WV 25305-0330
304-558-7010

Guaranty Agency
Pennsylvania Higher Education
   Assistance Agency
1200 North Seventh Street
Harrisburg, PA 17102-1444
717-720-2860, 800-692-7392

WISCONSIN

LEAPP
Higher Educational Aids Board
PO Box 7885
Madison, WI 53707-7885
608-267-2206 (LEAPP)

Byrd
State Department of Public Instruction
125 S. Webster Street
PO Box 7841
Madison, WI 53707-7841
608-266-2364

Guaranty Agency
Great Lakes Higher Education Corp.
2401 International Lane
PO Box 7658
Madison, WI 53707
608-246-1800, 800-236-5900

WYOMING

LEAPP
Wyoming Community College
   Commission
2020 Carey Avenue
8th Floor
Cheyenne, WY 82002
307-777-7763

Byrd
State Department of Education
Hathaway Building
2300 Capitol Avenue
2nd Floor
Cheyenne, WY 82002-0050
307-777-6265

Guaranty Agency
Sallie Mae
PO Box 6180
Indianapolis, IN 46206
317-849-6510, 800-428-9250

Additional State Grant, Scholarship, and Guaranty Agencies

AMERICAN SAMOA

LEAPP, Byrd
American Samoa Community College
Board of Higher Education
PO Box 2609
Pago Pago, American Samoa
96799-2609

FEDERATED STATES OF MICRONESIA, MARSHALL ISLANDS

Byrd
Federated States of Micronesia
1725 N Street N.W.
Washington, DC 20036
202-223-4383
Republic of the Marshall Islands
RMI Scholarship Grant and
Loan Board
PO Box 1436
3 Lagoon Road
Majuro, MH 96960
692-625-3108

GUAM

LEAPP, Byrd
University of Guam
303 University Drive
Mangilao, Guam 96923
671-735-2287 (LEAPP)
671-475-0457 (Byrd)

NORTHERN MARIANA ISLANDS

LEAPP
Northern Marianas College
PO Box 1250
Saipan, MP 96950
670-234-6128

Byrd
State Board of Public Education
   School System
Commonwealth of the Northern
   Mariana Islands
PO Box 1370 CK
Saipan, MP 96950

PUERTO RICO

LEAPP
Council on Higher Education
PO Box 19900
San Juan, PR 00910-1900
787-724-7100

Byrd
Department of Education
PO Box 759
Hato Rey, PR 00919
787-758-2200

REPUBLIC OF PALAU

LEAPP, Byrd
Palau Community College Office of
   Admission and Financial Aid
PO Box 9
Koror, Republic of Palau, TT 96940
680-488-1003

VIRGIN ISLANDS

LEAPP, Byrd
Department of Education/Virgin
   Islands Board of Education
Federal Programs
No 44-46 Kongens Gade
Charlotte Amalie
St Thomas, VI 00801
340-774-4546 (LEAPP)
340-774-0100 (Byrd)

Independent *529 Plan*

GUARANTEED TUITION
at AMERICA'S PRIVATE COLLEGES

A Better Way to Pay for Private College

Do you know how you will pay for your child's or grandchild's college education? Climbing at a rate of about 6 percent annually, tuition costs have more than tripled over the past twenty years. Today, as the price of a four-year college education continues to escalate, thousands of potential students may presume private colleges and universities are out of reach because they lack sufficient funds to foot the bill.

Planning for a child's college education may be one of the most significant financial decisions your family ever makes.

Now there's a new way to pay for private college that can help you afford an education that may have previously seemed out of reach. Independent 529 Plan is the first private college-sponsored, national, prepaid 529 plan. Independent 529 Plan gives you a unique new tool to help make your child's or grandchild's college education more affordable by allowing you to lock in tuition costs at less than today's price.

This innovative new way to pay for college offers the security of a guarantee against tuition inflation, freedom from market risk, and the flexibility of a national program—all free from federal taxes.

BEST PRODUCTS *2003* AWARD
BusinessWeek

Enroll Today! • www.ind529review.org • 1-888-718-7878

Independent 529 Plan Puts a Private College Education Within Your Reach

Independent 529 Plan is the first tax-advantaged program designed specifically to help you finance a private college education. Independent 529 Plan takes the risk and worry out of saving for a child's future college education.

Independent 529 Plan operates on a simple principle: in return for prepaying college costs, participating institutions carry the risk and protect you from future tuition increases. The tuition you purchase today is guaranteed to satisfy costs at the time your child enrolls. So if you purchase a half-year of tuition today, you get a half-year of tuition in the future. You lock in that half-year of tuition, no matter how much tuition rises or what happens in the investment markets.

To make the program even more attractive, each member college also offers a discount. This increases your savings even more by allowing you to lock in costs at less than today's price. Each college sets its own discount rate, but it will never be less than a half-percent per year, and it applies only to the amount of tuition prepurchased. Participating colleges can adjust the discount rate annually with respect to future purchases.

> *If you purchase a half-year of tuition today, you get a half-year of tuition in the future— no matter how much tuition rises or what happens in the investment markets.*

How It Works

With Independent 529 Plan, you prepay a percentage of tuition by purchasing certificates. When your child enrolls at a member college, you can use the certificate to pay for the percentage of tuition that you previously purchased. Once you've purchased a certificate, it must be held for a minimum of three years and redeemed within thirty years. Here's an example of how it works:

Let's suppose the college your child will eventually attend has a current tuition of $20,000 per year. If you prepay $20,000 today to cover one year of tuition, that amount will cover one year of tuition ten years from now— even though the projected cost at that time is $32,578 (using a 5 percent annual tuition rate increase). By prepaying, you save $12,578, and that savings is federal tax-free.

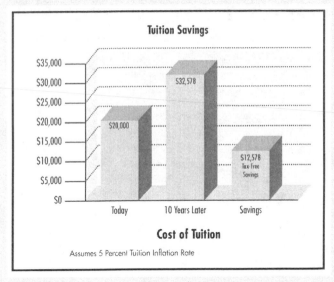

In addition to locking in costs, participating colleges and universities also offer a discount on the current tuition rate, so you save even more. Continuing with our example, the discount increases your savings from $12,578 to $14,758.

In this example, when your child enrolls ten years after the certificate purchase, a full year of tuition will cost you $17,820 (your $20,000 certificate minus the 1 percent discount), when others without Independent 529 Plan will be paying the full $32,578.

The bottom line: you will be paying about 55 percent—or just a little over half—of what someone without Independent 529 Plan is paying for the same education.

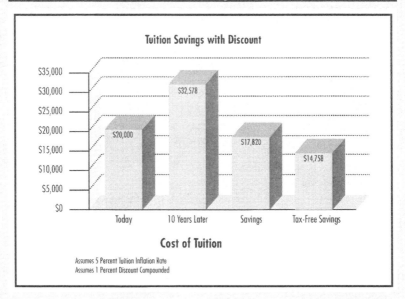

Tuition Savings with Discount

Assumes 5 Percent Tuition Inflation Rate
Assumes 1 Percent Discount Compounded

Assuming that private college tuition inflation continues at a rate of at least 5 percent per year and a median Independent 529 Plan annual discount rate of 1 percent, it's like earning a 6 percent return each year—tax-free. Of course, it may vary based on actual tuition increases and the discount rate at the college the child eventually attends.

Tracking Your Progress

When you open your Independent 529 Plan account, you'll have the opportunity to select five "sample" colleges to monitor. Each quarter you will receive a statement that displays the value of your account in terms of accumulated tuition benefit based on your five "sample" colleges.

While designation of a particular college as a benchmark has no bearing on admission to that school, it's a good way to illustrate where you are in terms of your goal. The five selections can be changed at anytime, so you can view the tuition value you've purchased at any of the participating institutions in the plan.

And while you don't have to choose the college in advance, you are locking in tuition costs at all the participating colleges.

The Advantages of Independent 529 Plan

Independent 529 Plan offers families like yours the advantage you need to make your child's private education achievable:

Guarantee Against Tuition Inflation

Tuition certificates are guaranteed by the colleges to retain their value no matter how much tuition rises or what happens in the investment markets. The plan offers you significant estate tax and gift benefits, and you pay no individual fees or charges with respect to your account.

Freedom from Market Risk

Unlike investment accounts, there is no market risk with Independent 529 Plan. By prepaying college tuition costs, you transfer the investment risk to the participating colleges and universities. Colleges are willing to do this because they can pool resources, spread the risk over time, and anticipate investment gains. In exchange, you lock in future tuition at less than today's price. If you prepay a percentage of tuition today, you get that same percentage tomorrow—no matter what the actual cost.

Independent 529 Plan at a Glance

- Prepay future private college tuition
- Lock in costs
- Free from federal taxes
- Enroll at any time
- Add to your account at any time
- No special eligibility requirements
- No income limits for participation
- Participating colleges pay all fees related to the program
- Certificates redeemable at any of the participating schools

More than 230 of the finest private colleges and universities across the nation are already participating, with more joining all the time.

Flexibility

Because every family's needs are different, Independent 529 Plan offers a number of ways to participate—from prepaying the full cost of several years to paying a set amount each month. The more and earlier you prepay, the greater the percentage of tuition you can lock in at less than today's price. However, you can also start small by contributing as little as $25 a month as long as a minimum of $500 is accumulated within two years.

Overall contribution limits to Independent 529 Plan are designed to cover the tuition and fees for five years at the most expensive college or university in the plan (which was $137,500 for the 2003–2004 school year). In addition to opening an account for a named beneficiary, you can open an account in the name of a trust, estate, or business for a scholarship for unnamed beneficiaries.

National in Scope

There are already more than 230 colleges and universities across the nation participating, offering a wide variety of choices to fit the talents and interests of every student. New member institutions are signing up all the time, giving your future student even more choices.

New schools joining Independent 529 Plan will retroactively honor certificates by all current holders. If a school withdraws from the plan (none have to date), it would continue to honor all certificates generated during and prior to the time of its participation.

All Federal Tax-Free

The increase in value between the amount of original purchase and the amount of tuition for which the certificate is redeemed is federal tax-free. Certificates are in the name of the child—not a college—and can be applied at any participating institution, including colleges and universities that join after the certificate was originally purchased.

No Special Eligibility Requirements, No Income Limits for Participation

There are no special eligibility requirements to take advantage of Independent 529 Plan. And there are no income limits for participation. If you are an adult U.S. resident who wants to help fund a private college education for children, grandchildren or any loved one, you are eligible.

Significant Estate and Gift Tax Benefits

Independent 529 Plan offers you significant estate and gift tax benefits that reduce the taxable value of your estate. Contributions to Independent 529 Plan are completed gifts and $11,000 annual exclusions may be used. This reduces the taxable value of your estate, while you retain complete control of the account. If you are married, your spouse may elect to split the gifts made to purchase a tuition certificate for a beneficiary, thereby doubling the amount of the annual gift tax exclusion—from $11,000 to $22,000.

Like all 529 Plans, Independent 529 Plan enjoys the benefit of a federal five-year-averaging provision. You can elect to treat up to $55,000 ($110,000 if married and filing jointly) as having been made in five equal gifts over a five-year period. If you contribute more than $55,000 in one year, the excess would be a taxable gift in the year of contribution.

Independent 529 Plan also features high contribution limits. For the 2003–2004 program year, the maximum lifetime contribution limit was $137,500, which would cover the cost for five years at the highest-priced participating institution.

No Entry Fees, No Annual Fees, No Exit Fees

All costs of administering the program, managing the assets, and running the Tuition Plan Consortium office are paid for by an annual management fee, which is picked up by the member colleges. That means that you pay no fees, and your entire contribution is applied directly to tuition.

With average annual tuition increases of 6 percent and fees for 529 savings plans in the 2 percent-per-year range, those customers would have to earn an approximate 8 percent return to equal the value of Independent 529 Plan. And for a family using investment vehicles outside of a 529 plan tax-free bubble, the equivalent return would have to be well into the double digits to match the value of Independent 529 Plan.

When Should I Open an Independent 529 Plan Account?

Even if your child is years away from college, the time to open an account is now! The earlier you start, the greater the percentage of tuition you can lock in at less than today's price. So while Independent 529 Plan doesn't guarantee your child admission, it does guarantee significant savings over the ever-rising cost of tuition.

What if My Child Doesn't Want to Go to College?

Even if your child chooses not to go to college, you have several options. You can leave the account open for future use—for up to 30 years. You can also change the beneficiary to another "member of the family," within the broadly defined 529 rules—even yourself!

Another option is to take a refund after a one-year waiting period, which will be adjusted for fund performance. As with any 529 program, if you do not use the money for qualified higher-education expenses, any increase in the value of your initial purchase amounts (the difference between your contribution amount and the amount refunded) will be subject to federal income tax as well as an additional 10 percent tax.

If you take a refund, rather than redeem your certificate for its intended purpose, the refund will be adjusted based on the net performance of the Program Trust, subject to a maximum return of 2 percent per annum and a maximum loss of 2 percent per annum.

What Makes Independent 529 Plan Unique?

Independent 529 Plan provides the same income, gift, and estate tax advantages as other 529 college savings plans. However, while most other 529 plans require you to assume some financial risk or settle for a relatively modest guaranteed rate of return, contributors to Independent 529 Plan do not assume tuition inflation or investment risk.

Some state prepaid 529 plans have been closed to new customers, and several more are financially troubled. Independent 529 Plan avoids a serious structural flaw that has crippled the state programs. Independent 529 Plan falls under the direct obligation of the participating colleges; if investment returns fall short, these colleges are still obligated. The state colleges have no similar obligation to underwrite the state programs.

With mutual funds and other college savings options, you invest your money in stocks or other securities in the hope that your returns, minus any taxes you might have to pay, will enable you to meet your goals. You may worry that the market will turn, just when you need the funds for college. Because Independent 529 Plan guarantees a distinct tuition benefit at each member college when you purchase a certificate, you don't have to risk your money in volatile investment markets to keep up with rising college costs.

While some savvy (and lucky) investors may be able to do better on their own, many families are drawn to the security offered by Independent 529 Plan, which takes the worry out of planning and saving for a child's education.

What if My Child Goes to a Nonmember College?

Additional colleges are joining Independent 529 Plan all the time, offering many choices for your family. However, if your child goes to a college or university that is not participating in Independent 529 Plan, you have several options. Funds may be withdrawn tax-free if the funds are either:

- transferred to another Section 529 "qualified tuition program" (including those that are state-sponsored) within sixty days of withdrawal, or

- changed to another beneficiary among certain family members specified in Section 529 within sixty days of withdrawal.

In addition to these options, you can also take a refund. If the proceeds are used for qualified higher-education expenses, then the earnings portion of the refunded money is still free from federal income tax and from the 10 percent federal excise tax. Independent 529 Plan's refund value is equal to the actual investment return, but it is capped at 2 percent per year on the upside and with loss protection at 2 percent per year on the downside.

Administered by the Country's Leading 529 Manager

Tuition Plan Consortium has entered into an agreement with TIAA-CREF Tuition Financing Inc. to provide administrative, service, and marketing support to the program.

TIAA-CREF is the nation's largest pension fund manager with over $300 billion in assets under management. Currently, TIAA-CREF manages twelve state-sponsored 529 plans in addition to Independent 529 Plan.

Why Pay Tomorrow's Price When You Can Pay Less Than Today's?

As college costs keep going up and up, Independent 529 Plan offers a solution to remove some of the financial pressures and make a private college education achievable. If you think your child may be destined for a private college, if you are a private college alum and would like your child to benefit from a private college education, or if the idea of minimizing financial risk and locking in costs is appealing, Independent 529 Plan may be right for you.

To learn more about Independent 529 Plan or to enroll, visit www.ind529review.org or call toll-free at 1-888-718-7878.

Hundreds of Participating Private Colleges and Counting

Independent 529 Plan includes a wide range of private colleges and universities to fit the talents and interests of all students when they're ready to select a college. Member institutions include research universities, traditional liberal arts colleges, women's colleges, religiously-affiliated colleges, historically Black colleges, and technically-oriented institutions.

Alabama
Birmingham-Southern College
Faulkner University
Mobile, University of
Samford University

Arkansas
Hendrix College
Lyon College

California
California Lutheran University
Claremont McKenna College
Harvey Mudd College
Mills College
Mount Saint Mary's College

Occidental College
Pepperdine University
Pitzer College
Point Loma Nazarene University
Pomona College
Redlands, University of
Saint Mary's College of California
San Diego, University of
Stanford University
University of LaVerne
University of the Pacific
University of San Diego
Westmont College
Whittier College

Enroll Today! • *www.ind529review.org* • *1-888-718-7878*

Colorado
Colorado College
Regis University

Connecticut
Fairfield University
Wesleyan University

District of Columbia
American University
Catholic University of America
George Washington University

Florida
Jacksonville University
Miami, University of
Rollins College
Saint Leo University

Georgia
Agnes Scott College
Berry College
Clark Atlanta University
Emory University
LaGrange College
Mercer University
Oglethorpe University
Spelman College
Wesleyan College

Hawaii
Chaminade University of Honolulu

Idaho
Northwest Nazarene University

Illinois
Augustana College
Bradley University
Chicago, University of
Illinois Institute of Technology
Knox College
Lake Forest College
Monmouth College
Olivet Nazarene University

Indiana
Butler University
DePauw University
Earlham College

Franklin College of Indiana
Rose-Hulman Institute of Technology
Saint Mary's College
Evansville, University of
Notre Dame, University of
Valparaiso University

Iowa
Buena Vista University
Central College
Clarke College
Dordt College
Grinnell College
Graceland University
Loras College
Luther College
Northwestern College
Waldorf College
Wartburg College

Kentucky
Centre College

Louisiana
Centenary College of Louisiana
Dillard University
Tulane University

Maryland
Notre Dame of Maryland, College of
Goucher College
Loyola College in Maryland
Mount Saint Mary's College
McDaniel College

Massachusetts
Amherst College
Berklee College of Music
Boston University
Clark University
Gordon College
Hampshire College
Massachusetts Institute of Technology
Mount Holyoke College
Smith College
Springfield College
Wellesley College
Wheaton College

Carnegie Mellon University
Chatham College
Dickinson College
Franklin & Marshall College
Gettysburg College
Grove City College
Immaculata University
Juniata College
La Salle University
Marywood University
Moravian College
Muhlenberg College
Saint Francis University
Thiel College
Ursinus College
Waynesburg College
Westminster College
York College of Pennsylvania

South Carolina
Charleston Southern University
Columbia College
Converse College
Furman University
Presbyterian College
Wofford College

South Dakota
Augustana College

Tennessee
Belmont University
Carson-Newman College
Lambuth University
Rhodes College
Trevecca Nazarene University
University of the South
Vanderbilt University

Texas
Abilene Christian University
Austin College

Baylor University
Dallas Baptist University
Dallas, University of
Hardin-Simmons University
Lubbock Christian University
Mary Hardin-Baylor, University of
Rice University
St. Edward's University
St. Mary's University
Southern Methodist University
Southwestern University
Texas Christian University
Trinity University

Vermont
Middlebury College
Saint Michael's College

Virginia
Bridgewater College
Eastern Mennonite University
Hampden-Sydney College
Hollins University
Mary Baldwin College
Randolph-Macon Woman's College
Richmond, University of
Shenandoah University
Sweet Briar College
Virginia Wesleyan College

Washington
Pacific Lutheran University
Seattle Pacific University
Whitworth College

West Virginia
West Virginia Wesleyan College

Wisconsin
Lakeland College
Lawrence University
Ripon College